GOVERNANCE
for GROWTH *in* INDIA

Born on 15 October 1931, at Rameswaram in Tamil Nadu, **Dr Avul Pakir Jainulabdeen Abdul Kalam** specialized in aeronautical engineering from Madras Institute of Technology. Dr Kalam is one of the most distinguished scientists of India and has received honorary doctorates from forty-five universities and institutions in India and abroad. He has been awarded the Padma Bhushan (1981), the Padma Vibhushan (1990) and India's highest civilian award, the Bharat Ratna (1997). He has also received the King Charles II medal (2007), the Woodrow Wilson Award (2008), the Hoover Award (2008) and the International Von Kármán Wings Award (2009), among other international accolades.

Dr Kalam became the eleventh President of India on 25 July 2002. His focus and greatest ambition is to find ways to transform India into a developed nation.

GOVERNANCE
for **GROWTH** *in* **INDIA**

A.P.J. ABDUL KALAM

Published by
Rupa Publications India Pvt. Ltd 2014
161-B/4, Gulmohar House,
Yusuf Sarai Community Centre,
New Delhi 110049

Sales centres:
Bengaluru Chennai
Hyderabad Kolkata Mumbai

Copyright © APJM Nazema Maraikayar 2015

The views and opinions expressed in this book are the author's own
and the facts are as reported by him which have been verified to the
extent possible, and the publishers are not in any way liable for the same.

All rights reserved.
No part of this publication may be reproduced, transmitted,
or stored in a retrieval system, in any form or by any means,
electronic, mechanical, photocopying, recording or otherwise,
without the prior permission of the publisher.

P-ISBN: 978-81-291-3260-4
E-ISBN: 978-81-291-3381-6

Twenty-second impression 2026

25 24 23 22

Printed in India

This book is sold subject to the condition that it shall not, by way
of trade or otherwise, be lent, resold, hired out, or otherwise circulated,
without the publisher's prior consent, in any form of binding or cover
other than that in which it is published.

Contents

Introduction   *vii*

Igniting the Faith of the Voter   1
The Role of the Youth in Governance   10
Creative Leadership: The Essence of Good Governance   26
Inclusive Growth for Good Governance   44
E-governance for Transparent Societies   54
The Right to Information in Governance   70
The Effects of Corruption   78
Public Audit and Good Governance   87
Transparency in Defence Missions   101
Governance for Every Citizen   114
The Vision for a New India   126

Introduction

Vote for the Nation

I was at Ropar, Punjab, on 20 March 2014 to address and interact with some students. I met a large gathering of young boys and girls. While I was entering the venue, a group of students—two girls and four boys—hailing from different states, approached me and said they had an important question and that I should answer it before I started my address and interaction.

The question that was put forth to me was: 'Sir, wherever we go, to any part of the country, be it on study tours or excursions or on leisure trips, we interact with the youth of that place. Many of them are our age, eighteen years and above. When we discuss our voting rights with them, most of them say that they will not vote as they think nobody deserves to lead us as Members of Parliament or Members of the Legislative Assembly. We, too, feel the same way and have decided not to vote in the forthcoming elections. Sir, please tell us whether we have taken the right decision?'

I told them, 'Dear friends, I do not agree with you completely. In my eighty plus years of age, I have seen many parliamentary and assembly elections, and at each one I have voted for the right kind of person. At every election, there are new candidates and sitting MPs and MLAs contest too. You have to choose the best candidate among them, based on their work and contribution to society. Many a time, the contribution is visible in the constituency from where they are contesting and there is also a record of their overall performance in the Parliament/Assembly. Information on their performance is also available through the media and the Internet. Based on the candidate's credentials, you can discuss among yourselves and select the best performing, cleanest candidate, and vote for that person.

'Remember, your "right to vote" is precious and to exercise your franchise is essential. You have a great opportunity to select the right person to represent you in the Parliament or in the Assembly. That means you, as a young citizen, are helping the nation to evolve a good government at the centre or state. The nation will be grateful to you if you cast your vote and choose the right candidate.'

This book has been written to examine the challenges we face as a democracy and to find some solutions so that we can all travel together on the road towards good governance, the end of corruption and a truly empowered nation. I hope every youth and every citizen will be inspired to participate fully in the democratic process after reading this book and that it also answers some of the questions posed by my young friends at Ropar, Punjab.

Igniting the Faith of the Voter

Life has to be built on a great ideal.

Parliamentary Democracy

The tradition of democracy is not alien to India. Their importance in our history can be traced back to the ancient period when Sabhas and Samitis were two highly respected institutions in our village republics and performed functions similar to those of the popular representative bodies of today. Our choice of a democratic political system after achieving independence was, therefore, a continuation of an ethos that had always been there.

We are proud to be the world's largest thriving parliamentary democracy. What amazes the world perhaps is the sagacity and maturity of the Indian voter who has always tried to exercise the mandate conscientiously and enthusiastically, proving time and again that the people are sovereign and the power flows from them.

Elections and the Youth of India

India is considered to be one of the youngest nations in the world in terms of its demographics. We have about 600 million youth and about 160 million of them are registered voters. In the future, the number of youth voters will only grow progressively. In this scenario, it is necessary to ensure that the youth are an integral and vibrant part of the democratic process. How do we motivate the youth to be partners in elections? How do we motivate the ones who don't vote normally due to various reasons?

> The youth of India want to see elected members as their role models through their performance in the Parliament or State Assembly, and also in the way they lead their lives.
>
> They definitely expect the elected representatives to ensure that the performance of the Parliament and State Assemblies are never disturbed or halted. For them, this action of non-performance is a crime. Above all, the youth of the nation want their representatives to follow the mission of developmental politics.

In this context, I would like to examine what changes we can bring about in the way we conduct our electoral process. We should also assess the expectations we have from the men and women we elect.

Constituency Manifesto

I would like to share with you my experience of interacting with the newly elected members of the legislative assembly of Karnataka in 2008 at the Indian Institute of Management, Bangalore. Before the interaction, I designed a questionnaire for the legislative members regarding their constituency development plans. This questionnaire was well publicized by the media, who said that I should not expect any substantial response from the members. However, to my pleasure and the media's surprise, I received more than a hundred responses, each well thought out and precisely planned and they reached me well before the interaction, despite a relatively short notice.

Let me share the questionnaire here.

1. What change would you bring in your constituency after 2.5 years and after 5 years?
2. Do you have plans to realize 100 per cent literacy in your constituency? If so, you may indicate your plan.
3. With what skill and expertise will you empower the members of your constituency to increase the per capita income by at least two times?
4. Do you have a plan to plant at least 100,000 trees in your constituencies?
5. How will you rejuvenate the water bodies in your constituencies and activate their inlet and outlet?

6. How will you facilitate sanitary facilities in your constituency with adequate water supply and its management?
7. Will you plan for multi-cropping and also for the plantation of Jatropha in the wasteland in your constituency?
8. How will you make your constituency free from power cuts and power shortage by using renewable energy sources?
9. Will you pave the way for peaceful and prosperous livelihoods of the citizens in your constituency?

When I had gone through the responses, I found that the members were keen on the development of their constituencies in their tenure and to make a difference through their developmental politics. On the other hand, rarely had any political party asked for such a micro plan at the constituency level from their own members, except representations which came now and then from the people.

Can the Election Commission suggest to the parties to include constituency development plans as a part of the overall manifesto of the party with time-bound targets? This will empower the voters to make their own judgements based on the developmental needs and deliverables of their regions.

State Funding of Elections

In the same interaction with the legislators of the Karnataka Assembly, I administered this oath that all the participating members took:

Oath for Legislators

1. I am proud to be a member of the legislative assembly/council of Karnataka of high tradition.
2. The welfare and happiness of the citizens of my constituency come first always and every time.
3. I will work hard to make my constituency fully literate, healthy, empowered, happy and poverty free.
4. I will not allow any discrimination in my constituency by way of religion, language, caste or creed.
5. I will be transparent in all my actions and become a role model for all the citizens of my constituency.
6. I will celebrate the success of the citizens of my constituency.
7. My constituency is my life and my state and the nation is my soul.
8. I will work with integrity and succeed with integrity.

After the administration of the oath, I asked for questions from the members. One young member said, 'Dr Kalam, we all took the oath right now and promised to work with integrity and succeed with integrity. That is all fine, we will try to do that. But do you know how much I spent to become a legislative member?'

I didn't have an answer so he continued, '₹80 lakh.' He then asked me, 'How can I work with integrity and succeed with integrity?'

My only answer at that time to the question was that the state has to fund the election expenses of the candidates and the accounts should be scrutinized by the Election Commission. But in the present system, with over fourteen candidates on an average contesting for each seat, is this practical? In that case, is the two-party system something we need to consider seriously?

The Two-Party System

Here I would like to recall my suggestion to the Honourable Members of Parliament during my farewell address to them in 2007 before completing my tenure as President. I mentioned that India has to eventually graduate to a two-party political system. There was lot of criticism of that suggestion and none of the political parties liked that idea. What I meant was that it may mean two strictly defined coalitions with pre-poll affiliations and a clear-cut development agenda agreed upon by all the partners and publicly debated over the electronic media.

We are witnessing an election in one or other part of the country every now and then. I suggested the need for concurrent elections for State Assemblies and the Lok Sabha to minimize the time and resources spent on elections and provide time to the representatives for the development of the constituency in a coordinated way.

Of course, these suggestions elicited varied responses from the political parties. We need to further discuss and debate how we can evolve an election system which will bring about a stable government and which can fulfil the aspirations of the people and take the nation towards development.

We also have to study and analyse the various forms of democratic election systems such as proportional representation so that people are enthused to participate in a big way to elect their representatives and recall their representatives when they don't perform.

Simplifying the Voting Process

With the rapid progress of information technology and communication infrastructure in the nation, it is time we look at how technology can be coupled with secure systems to simplify the voting process. With the introduction of a unique identification number for each citizen, the Election Commission can consider the possibility of creating a system for Internet/mobile-based voting, which is fool-proof and devoid of any loopholes. Moreover, with almost one mobile phone existing for every two Indians, we can further use technology to evolve a system for secure and reliable mobile-based voting.

I am sure this technology interface will not only save costs but also enable larger participation and promote safety, secrecy and transparency. The same technology can be used to facilitate easier access to information about the candidates and their profiles, using systems such as emails, IVRS (Interactive

Voice Response System) based platforms or through SMS (short messaging service), MMS (Multi Media Service) as well as social media.

Role of the Members of Parliament

The Parliament is a pivotal institution of democracy. But it has to revitalize itself in order to become a vibrant and progressive fortress of democracy. The parliamentarians' role, therefore, assumes tremendous significance and it is essential that Members of Parliament live up to the aspirations and ideals for which they have been elected.

Our polling processes have been, sometimes, under severe strain with certain fatal incidents. The compulsions of incremental numbers and the alleged tradability of legislative seats won perhaps through means dubious and undemocratic, have many a time created doubts about our democratic system in the public eye. When politics degrades itself to political adventurism, the nation is put on the calamitous road to inevitable disaster and ruination. Let us not risk it. It is time for all of us to introspect and live up to the expectations that were enshrined so diligently and optimistically in our Constitution so that India sustains itself and grows as a mature, healthy, vibrant, democratic nation.

In every action of our Members of Parliament, the 600 million youth in our country who are below twenty-five years of age should find inspiration—great leaders who can be their role models and who can bring a dynamic change in politics and fulfil developmental missions. The Members of Parliament owe it to the voters to meet their expectations. The ascending trajectory of the nation's progress cannot be ensured unless we put the nation above ourselves.

The Parliament needs to mount a mission to identify and scrap the complex old laws and administrative procedures which are hindering a growth-oriented economy. This will give hope to a large section of people. The people need to develop more trust in their leaders and only the Members of Parliament can bring about this change. Their name is waiting to be written in the important pages of the history of India.

Let us show to ourselves and the world the maturity we have gained in our politics, and how we can utilize that for the sustained development of our nation. We will strive to build an India that is vibrant, vigilant, safe and secular. I am sure that this is well within our capability and we can achieve it if we really strive towards it.

The Role of the Youth in Governance

*If we do not talk differently,
we shall not think differently.*
~Tony Judt

Dear young people of India, I would like to put forward to you four questions. If you are able to answer these four questions and understand the principles behind them, you will succeed in all your endeavours. And if *you* succeed, India will succeed in becoming a developed nation, where good governance is available to all its people.

The four questions are as follows:

1. How do you transform a child into a leader?
2. How do you nurture the seeds to help it grow into a bigger mission?
3. How do you identify what is unique in you?
4. What are the criteria for achieving success?

I would like to recall the inspiring advice of Swami Vivekananda: *How has all the knowledge in the world been gained but by the concentration of the power of the mind? The world is ready to give up its secret if we only know how to knock, how to give it the necessary blow. The strength and force of the blow come through concentration. There is no limit to the power of the human mind. The more concentrated it is, the more power is brought to bear on one point: that is the secret.*

This thought has indeed influenced my conscience and I would suggest that the education system develop in the minds of young people this faith in the power of the mind. At the same time, the youth of India, too, must practice this in all their actions.

> History has proven that those who dare to imagine the impossible are the ones who break all human limitations. In every field of human endeavour, whether science, medicine, sports, the arts, or technology, the names of the people who imagined the impossible and achieved greatness are engraved in our history. By breaking the limits of their imagination, they changed the world.

The Leadership Quality

Every one of us has gone through various phases of education from childhood to our professional life. Let's visualize a scene where there is a child, a teenager, an adult and a leader. How does each one react to a particular situation? The situation is human need. The child asks, 'What can you do for me?' The teenager says, 'I want to do it alone.' The adult proclaims, 'Let us do it together.' The leader asks, 'What can I do for you?'

The question—the first question I asked you—is how do we transform a child into a leader; the transformation of 'What can you do for me?' to 'What can I do for you?' The challenge in our society, from the home to the school and the workplace, is that we need visionary leaders at every level who have the capability to inspire others. We need to bring out the best in our youth and for this, a leader has to be a good teacher. I am sure the creativity and dedication of our youth will emerge by the integrated efforts of parents, teachers and leaders in all walks of life.

Nurturing the Seeds

Let me recall an incident in the year 2001, when I was teaching a course on 'Societal Transformation Using Technology' at Anna University, Chennai. I was invited by the Presidency College of Chennai to interact with their students. When I reached the venue, I saw more than 1,500 students crowding the hall. It was very tough to reach the dais. After I finished my lecture, 'Vision Elevates the Nation', I received a number of questions from the students, which I answered. When I was leaving the hall, a young student suddenly pushed himself forward from the crowd and thrust a crumpled paper into my hand. I put the paper into my pocket and read it in the car on my way back to Anna University. My heart was uplifted by the power of the message that T. Saravanan, who was doing his MPhil in Presidency College at that time, had written. I would like to share the contents of the letter with you, since it is relevant to the subject we are discussing. The letter went like this:

Dear Kalam Sir,

The full power of the banyan tree is equal to the power in the seeds of the tree. In a way both of us, you and I, are the same, but we exhibit our talents in different forms. A few of the seeds become banyan trees but many seeds die as saplings without ever becoming a tree. Due to certain circumstances and environmental conditions, many seeds get damaged and become part of the soil as manure, helping new seeds to become trees.

You have worked for the country and helped many scientists, engineers and knowledge workers. Can you tell me how you ensured that their abilities were not wasted or their growth was not stunted prematurely, like the banyan seeds that never became trees? In your service, what is the percentage of success you can claim?

I suitably answered Saravanan and added how much joy his letter had given me. Since he wanted to know the percentage of success, I replied that it would have been about 60 per cent at least. But this 60 per cent emerged out of the 100 per cent who worked for the projects. Even though some could not reach their full potential due to different circumstances, each contribution was valuable and welcome—the seeds that did not grow into trees were important for the growth of new trees.

> The message I would like to give is this: the seeds of the banyan tree are indeed like the citizens of the nation. Democracy and good governance have the power to provide equal opportunity to every citizen to grow and to perform—to become trees of their own. Every citizen therefore has the capacity to contribute to the vision of the country in his or her own way and, in the process, contribute to the success of few. And this can grow in geometric proportion and result in the success of the Indian nation, a success that may be shared by all Indian citizens. Let us nurture every seed. Nevertheless, seeds that become manure must not be treated any lesser than the seeds that become trees.

The You that is Unique

When you look around the room you are sitting in as you read this book, what do you see? Lights, electric bulbs. Immediately, your thoughts turn to Thomas Alva Edison, the inventor of the electric bulb and the electrical lighting system.

When you hear the sound of an aeroplane flying over your house, who do you think of? The Wright brothers, of course. They proved man can fly too.

When everybody considered sea travel only as a voyage, one person asked an important question during his trip from England to India by sea. He pondered why the horizon, where the sky and the sea meet, looks blue. His research resulted in groundbreaking work on the phenomenon of scattering of light. And for that, Sir C.V. Raman was awarded the Nobel Prize.

Can you name an Indian mathematician who did not have formal higher education but had an inexhaustible spirit and love for mathematics that led him to contribute enormously to mathematical research? This mathematician was Srinivasa Ramanujan, for whom every number was a divine manifestation. He was a genius whose work captivated the heart of the most outstanding Cambridge mathematician, Professor G.H. Hardy. In fact, it is not an exaggeration to say that it was Professor Hardy, Ramanujan's mentor, who discovered a great mathematician for the world.

There was a great lady of science, who is remembered for discovering radiation. She won not one, but two Nobel Prizes, one for physics and another for chemistry. Who was she? She was Madam Curie. She discovered radium and for several years researched the effects of radiation on the human system. The same radiation affected her and she sacrificed her life.

There was a great human being dedicated to the service of humanity and who was awarded the Nobel Peace Prize. Her motto was, 'Give, give and give, until it hurts.' She was Mother Teresa.

Why am I putting forth these examples? I have, so far, met seventeen million youth in my travels across the country. I have learnt that every youth wants to be unique. Each person has the potential and the ambition to do something that will change the world of science or arts or the society. You want to be YOU! But the world all around you is doing its best, day and night, to make you just like everybody else. At home you are asked by your parents to be like other children, and to score good marks like them. When you go to school, your teachers say that you must be at the top of the class. Wherever you go, people keep telling you that you have to be like somebody else. But dear young friends, how many of you would like to be uniquely *you*?

Like the great people whose examples I gave earlier, and many others like them, the challenge is that you have to fight the hardest battle that any human being can ever fight; and never stop fighting until you arrive at your destination: which is to be your own person!

How to Achieve Your Potential

How can you achieve your ambitions and unlock your potential? There are four proven steps:

- Having an aim in life before you are twenty years of age;
- Acquiring knowledge continuously;
- Working hard, with the aim to defeat any problem and to succeed, no matter what;
- Having enough willpower and confidence to achieve great deeds.

In this connection, let me recall these verses of the thirteenth-century Persian Sufi poet Jalaluddin Rumi:

I am born with potential.
I am born with goodness and trust.
I am born with ideas and dreams.
I am born with greatness.
I am born with confidence.
I am born with wings.
So, I am not meant for crawling,
I have wings, I will fly,
I will fly and fly.

My message to my young friends is that education gives you the wings to fly. Achievement comes when your conscious and subconscious mind believes: 'I will win'.

Each one of you must have 'Wings of Fire'. These wings will lead to knowledge which will, in turn, make you fly high—as a doctor, an engineer, a scientist, a teacher, a political leader, a bureaucrat, a diplomat or anything else you want to be.

If each of you develops the attitude of 'What can I give?' then the nation will be transformed. How can you do this? What can you give? Each of us can give three things for which we don't need wealth.

- If we go out of our homes—in cities or villages—we will find a number of clusters where some men and women may not know how to read and write. If each one of us take it as a mission to visit these homes and teach ten people how to read and write in a period of two to three months, we will be giving back to society through the learning process.
- In our home or place of work, or in a park, we can plant ten trees and nurture them. You have to realize that every mature tree gives 14 kg of oxygen in a year and absorbs 20 kg of carbon dioxide through the process of photosynthesis. Thus we can assist in creating a beautiful and pollution-free environment.
- In every government hospital, we see scenes during the visiting hours where patients receive relatives and friends. But there will be a few beds with aged patients or those who have no support, who are alone, with no one to visit them. If you carry flowers and fruits to them with a smile, reach out to such patients, God's love will flow through you to them.

Of course some of you may be blessed with wealth. Here I would like to relate the life story of a great human being who gave and gave. In 2007, I received a personal invitation to inaugurate the 100th year celebrations of Sree Sree Sivakumara Swamiji at Siddaganga Math. When I reached there, I saw a mammoth gathering of lakhs of devotees, who had congregated to greet the seer. Many political and spiritual leaders were also present. After every leader had spoken, Sree Sree Sivakumara Swamiji got up without any paper in his hand and gave an extempore lecture. I was astonished to see the scene. A hundred-year-old seer, standing erect, giving an extempore speech made me ask myself, how is this achievement possible? It is only because he has been giving and giving to the people through the creation of educational institutions, many orphanages and the feeding of thousands of needy people every day. His tireless mission of socio-economic service and the eradication of the evils of illiteracy and discrimination has uplifted many people in the region.

What is the India we wish to realize when our youth are motivated, educated and empowered?

The India We Visualize

- A nation where the rural and urban divide has reduced to a thin line.
- A nation where there is equitable distribution and adequate access to energy and water.

- A nation where the agriculture, industry and service sectors work together in symphony.
- A nation where education is not denied to any meritorious candidate because of societal or economic discrimination.
- A nation which is the best destination for talented scholars, scientists and investors.
- A nation where the best of healthcare is available to all.
- A nation where governance is responsive, transparent and corruption free.
- A nation where poverty has been totally eradicated, illiteracy removed and crimes against women and children are absent and none in the society feels alienated.
- A nation that is prosperous, healthy, secure, devoid of terrorism, peaceful and happy and continues on a sustainable growth path.
- A nation that is one of the best places in the world to live in and one that is proud of its leadership.

I would suggest that each one of us should select an important task pertaining to any of the ten pillars which I have described based on one's interests and core competence and work towards realizing some part of this vision.

Integrated Action for a Developed India

Our mission is to transform India into a developed nation and achieve the distinctive profile of India. There are five areas where India needs core competence:

- Agriculture and food processing
- Education and healthcare
- Information and communication technology
- Infrastructure: reliable and quality electric power, surface transport
- Self reliance in critical technologies

These five areas are closely inter-related and progress in these areas in a coordinated way will lead to self sufficiency in food, economic stability and the security of our nation.

For this to be a reality, the youth has to focus on inclusive governance. Let me focus now on how the youth can help in providing inclusive governance.

Governance for the Billions

> Friends, good governance is identified by the way it is proactive and responsive to the needs of the people and helps them lead a life that is morally upright, intellectually superior, and leads to an enriched quality of life.

This is possible by the acquisition of knowledge which will consequently lead to the overall enhancement of the quality of life of all Indian citizens.

I feel we need to evolve the Societal Grid—which comprises the Knowledge Grid, the Health Grid and the E-governance Grid—all feeding the PURA (Providing Urban Amenities to Rural Areas) Grid in order to achieve holistic development.

The Knowledge Grid will bring appropriate knowledge democratically to all citizens, empowering them and thereby ensuring the establishment of a knowledge society.

The Health Grid will ensure that the benefits of quality healthcare reach the needy people, enhancing the quality of life and increasing individual productivity, which, in turn, will help the nation develop faster.

The E-governance Grid will ensure transparency in government services, reaching all people uniformly, without any dilution of the quantum and the quality of services.

If these Grids help each other, then it will enhance the quality of services of the PURA Grid, which connects 600,000 villages. When villages are empowered, we can finally have inclusive growth.

Empowered villages ensure good and smart governance. The success stories which we have seen in our country gives me the confidence that the establishment of the Societal Grid model is possible.

Innovation will rest on the business model which we evolve around these Grids. Such a Grid will provide the people of the country the opportunity to choose a path that will not only guarantee success for themselves but also contribute towards the goal of transforming India into a developed nation.

Inclusive governance will bring societal transformation by promoting inclusive economic policies, thereby abandoning prohibitive and extractive economic policies. The nation can grow only by empowering its people to contribute in agriculture and industry and in the service sectors. This is possible by empowering them financially, and by providing them with the requisite skill, knowledge and technology. Inclusive economic policies will make India a globally competitive nation.

Only this approach will help in achieving a sustainable GDP growth for a decade in order to make India an economically developed nation.

An End to Corruption

In order to bring about inclusive governance, the first and foremost requirement is to build a corruption-free transparent society.

We belong to a society of 200 million families. Nearly every family has four members: father, mother and on an average two children.

I have a mission for the youth of the nation, that is, the daughter or son of the family. After all, corruption emanates from the home. It is estimated that 30 per cent of our Indian homes have indulged in some form of corruption. That means approximately 60 million houses may not be transparent in their dealings. In such a scenario, while the children should appreciate their parents if they are fully transparent in all their dealings, in cases where they are not, they should have the courage to say no to such practices. My conscience says, compared to any law against corruption, this movement of the youth against corruption will be much more effective.

How many of my friends will offer to become a participant in such a great mission of making the home transparent? If you make your home transparent, then you can certainly bring a transformation which ultimately leads to inclusive governance.

Oath for the Youth

- I will have a goal and work hard to achieve that goal. I realize that thinking small is a crime.
- I will work with integrity and succeed with integrity.
- I will be a good member of my family, a good member of the society, a good member of the nation and a good member of the world.

- I will always try to better someone's life, without any discrimination of caste, creed, language, religion or state. Wherever I am, the thought that will always come to my mind is, 'What can I give?'
- I will always protect and enhance the dignity of every human life without any bias.
- I will always remember the importance of time. My motto will be, 'Let not my winged days be spent in vain.'
- I will always work for a clean planet and for clean energy.
- As a youth of my nation, I will work with courage to achieve success in all my tasks and enjoy the success of others.
- I am as young as my faith and as old as my doubt. Hence, I will light the lamp of faith in my heart.
- My national flag flies in my heart and I will bring glory to my nation.

Creative Leadership: The Essence of Good Governance

*Before you do anything, stop and recall the face of
the poorest, most helpless, destitute person
you have seen and ask yourself,
'Is what I am about to do going to help him?'*
~Mahatma Gandhi

Leadership is the Essence of Good Governance

What are the characteristics of good leadership?

- A leader should be ready to give to others rather than expect others to give to him;
- A leader should be equipped to manage change;
- A leader should have nobility of heart;
- A leader should have vision and clear thinking, and the capacity to be a facilitator.

Creative Leadership: The Essence of Good Governance

How do we make the governance system of our country most effective in order to ensure the development of the nation and to sustain it as an economically developed, prosperous, happy and peaceful society? For that we need creative leadership in all segments of the governance of the nation.

I have seen three national programmes succeed with the help of creative and effective leadership despite several challenges: the space programme of ISRO (Indian Space Research Organization), the AGNI programme of DRDO (Defence Research and Development Organization) and PURA (Providing Urban Amenities to Rural Areas).

> In all these areas, I have seen that a true leader needs to be passionate, with the ability to travel on uncharted territory and courage to take quick and effective decisions. A true leader also needs nobility and honesty of vision.

Let me illustrate these characteristics through our national programmes.

Vision for Self-sufficiency in Food

The vision for India's Green Revolution was formed in the 1970s under the leadership of C. Subramaniam. With his visionary leadership, and with the scientific leadership of Nobel Laureate Dr Norman Borlaugh and Dr M.S. Swaminathan, and the active support of B. Sivaraman, Secretary Agriculture, in partnership with agricultural scientists and farmers, the team liberated India from the situation of what was called a 'ship to mouth existence'. Through an effort of historical magnitude, India attained near self-sufficiency in food through the 'seed to grain' mission. Because of the Green Revolution, the country is now able to produce over 236 million tonnes of food grain per year. Of course, farmers played a pivotal role in working alongside agricultural scientists to make this possible.

Political and scientific leadership has been able to build capacity among our scientists, researchers and farmers and so we are now taking up the mission of the Second Green Revolution which involves knowledge graduation from the characterization of soil to the matching of the seed with the composition of the fertilizer, effective water management and evolving pre-harvesting techniques for such conditions. Under this project, the domain of a farmer's work would enlarge from merely production of grains to food processing and marketing.

The Second Green Revolution will enable India to further increase its productivity in the agricultural sector. By 2020, India envisions the production of over 340 million tonnes of food grain in view of population growth and increased purchasing power. The increase in production would surmount many impeding factors such as reduced availability of land, shortage of water and reduction in availability of agricultural workforce. Our agricultural scientists and technologists, in partnership with farmers, have to work towards increasing the average productivity per hectare by three times of the present productivity. New technology would also be needed in the development of seeds that would ensure high yield even under constraints of water and land.

Passion to Realize a Vision

Now let me give you an example of how passion to realize a vision has facilitated the successful and on-time implementation of a two-billion-dollar metro-rail project by the managing director of a public sector organization.

The Delhi Metro Rail Project has opened up the potential of executing a fast transportation system throughout the country that uses high technology with reliability. Delhi, the capital of the country with over 20 million people, has the distinction of having a world-class metro rail with front-line technology.

The work on the metro rail commenced on 1 October 1998 and the first phase, with three lines covering 65 km, was completed by December 2005. Today, the overall route length of the Delhi Metro is around 190 km. Every day, the metro handles a minimum of two million passengers.

The Delhi Metro Rail Corporation has brought to the country the most advanced rail technologies available. The notable components of the Delhi Metro are: lightweight stainless steel, sleek, modern trains with pneumatic springs, regenerative braking, public information display, wide vestibules and automatic doors. The sophisticated coach technology, which was not available in the country so far, has been transferred to BEML (Bharat Earth Movers Ltd.), Bangalore, which is now in the process of assembling these trains with progressive indigenization. BEML is now in a position to meet the upcoming requirement of trains in other cities of the country.

E. Sreedharan, the then managing director of the Delhi Metro Rail Corporation, had ensured that all the scheduled sections were completed on or before the target date and within their respective budgets. This dedicated and transparent leadership, backed by professional competence, gave the nation one of the best transportation systems in the world at the most economical cost. E. Sreedharan has since been a recipient of many national and international awards. He has been in demand to undertake the development of metro systems in other countries, which he has politely declined due to his commitment to Indian programmes.

Mastering the Problem

In 1954-57, while I was studying aeronautical engineering at MIT (Madras Institute of Technology), during the third year of my course, I was assigned a project to design a low-level attack aircraft together with five other students. My design teacher Professor Srinivasan, the then Director of MIT, was our guide. A few weeks into the project, he reviewed the progress and declared my work to be disappointing. He didn't listen to any of my reasons for this to be so. I asked for a month's time to complete the task, but Professor Srinivasan told me, 'Young man, today is Friday afternoon. I give you three days. By Monday morning if I don't get the configuration design, your scholarship will be stopped.' This was a big jolt, as the scholarship was my lifeline, and I could not continue my studies without it. There was no other way out but to finish the task. All of us in the team worked round the clock. We didn't sleep that night, working on the drawing board and skipping our dinner. On Saturday, I took just an hour's break. On Sunday morning, as I had nearly completed the work, I felt someone's presence in my laboratory. It was the professor, studying my progress. After looking at my work, he patted me and hugged me affectionately. He said, 'I knew I was putting you under stress and asking you to meet a difficult deadline. You have done a great job in mastering the problem and emerging stronger.'

This experience made me understand the value of time and the ability to tackle a seemingly impossible problem by keeping a calm mind.

Travelling the Unexplored Path

I was fortunate to work with Professor Vikram Sarabhai for seven years. While working closely with him, I saw the dawn of the vision for the space programme in a one-page statement. Witnessing the evolution of this page, and to be a part of the team that worked ceaselessly for many years to realize this vision, has been a great learning experience for me. The famous vision statement of Professor Vikram Sarabhai made in the year 1970 states, 'India, with her mighty scientific knowledge and power house of young, should build her own huge rocket systems (satellite launch vehicles) and also build her own communication, remote sensing and meteorological spacecraft and launch from her own soil to enrich Indian life in satellite communication, remote sensing and meteorology. The projects selected in the space programme are designed to meet the societal needs.'

If I look at the original vision statement today, I am overwhelmed to see the results of this statement. Today, there are a total of 150 transponders in the geo-synchronous orbit for providing connectivity to the nation. Today, India can build any type of satellite launch vehicle or any type of spacecraft and launch them from Indian soil. India has launched Chandrayaan and the Mars Orbiter Mission. India has proved that through space science and technology, we can provide effective communication, resource mapping, disaster prediction and disaster management systems.

Now, I would like to illustrate how Dr Sarabhai could always travel the unexplored path.

It was the early 1960s. The founder of the Indian space research programme, along with his team, had located a place technically most suited for space research after considering several alternatives. The place was called Thumba in Kerala, and it was selected as it was near the magnetic equator and therefore ideally suited for ionospheric and electrojet research in the upper atmosphere.

The major challenge for Professor Sarabhai was to obtain permissions for the specific area. As was normal, he approached the Kerala government first. After the profiling of the land and the sea coast, the view was that thousands of fishing folk lived there, and the place had an ancient St Mary Magdalene Church, a Bishop's house and a school, so it would be very difficult to give this land out to the team. But the administration was willing to provide the programme land in an alternative area. The political system also opined that it would be a difficult situation, keeping in mind the existence of important institutions in that area and the welfare of the people who would have to be relocated in the process. However, it was suggested that Professor Sarabhai and his team approach the only person who could advise and help them: Rev Father Peter Bernard Pereira, who was the bishop of the region.

I still remember that Professor Sarabhai approached the bishop on a Saturday evening. The meeting between the two turned out to be historical. Many of us witnessed the event. The Rev Father exclaimed, 'Oh Vikram, you are asking for my children's abode, my abode and God's abode. How is that possible?' However, both of them had a unique quality—they could smile even in the most difficult of situations. Rev Father Pereira asked Professor Sarabhai to come to church on Sunday morning at nine.

When Professor Sarabhai went to the church with his team on Sunday, Father Pereira was reading from the Bible. After the prayers were over, the bishop invited Professor Sarabhai to come up to the front. He introduced him to the people: 'Dear children, here is a scientist, Professor Vikram Sarabhai. What do the sciences do? All of us experience it first-hand. Everything is made possible through science, including the construction of this church, the lights in it, the mike, which makes it possible for me to talk to you. The diagnosis and treatment of patients by doctors comes through the medical sciences. Science through technology enhances the comfort and quality of human life. And what do *I* do, as a preacher? I pray for you, for your well being, for your peace. In short, what Vikram is doing and what I am doing are the same thing: both science and spirituality seek the Almighty's blessings for the prosperity of the human body and mind.

'Dear children, Professor Vikram says that he will build within a year, near the sea coast, alternative facilities to what we now have. Now, dear children, can we give your abode, can we give my abode, can we give God's abode for a great scientific mission?' For a moment, there was total silence. Then the entire congregation got up and said 'Amen' so loudly that the whole church reverberated.

That was the church where we had our design centre and where we started rocket assembly, and the bishop's house was our scientists' working place. Later, TERLS (Thumba Equatorial Rocket Launching Station) led to the establishment of the VSSC

(Vikram Sarabhai Space Centre) and this was later transformed into multiple space centres throughout the country. Now the old church has become an important centre of learning, where thousands of people learn about the dynamic history of the space programme of India. Of course, the Thumba citizens were provided with a place of worship, an educational centre and other well-equipped facilities at an alternate place.

When I think of this event, I can see how enlightened spiritual and scientific leaders can work together. Of course, the birth of TERLS and then the VSSC gave the country the capability to launch vehicles, spacecraft and space applications that have accelerated social and economic development in India to unprecedented levels.

Today, Professor Vikram Sarabhai is not among us, neither is Rev Father Peter Bernard Pereira, but those who are will be responsible for the creation of several other programmes. They will become like the flowers described in the Bhagwad Gita:

See the flower,
how generously it distributes perfume and honey.
It gives to all, gives freely of its love.
When its work is done, it falls away quietly.
Try to be like the flower, unassuming despite all its qualities.

What a beautiful message about the purpose of human life.

Managing Successes and Failures

Leaders with great minds are always looking for the right people to steer a project. The right people are self-driven, self-motivated and have no need of constant monitoring. For innovation to flourish, we must respect zeal and sincerity, irrespective of age and experience.

Three decades ago, while I was working at ISRO, I had a learning experience that has stayed with me my entire life.

I was given a task by Professor Satish Dhawan, then the chairman of ISRO, to develop the first satellite launch vehicle, SLV-3, to put the Rohini satellite in orbit. This was one of the largest high-technology space programmes undertaken in 1973. The whole space technology community, men and women, were geared up for the task. Thousands of scientists, engineers and technicians worked relentlessly towards the realization of the first SLV-3 launch on 10 August 1979.

SLV-3 took off in the early hours and the first stage worked beautifully. But even though all the stage rockets and systems worked, the mission could not achieve its objectives, as the control system malfunctioned in the second stage. Instead of being placed in orbit, the Rohini satellite went into the Bay of Bengal. The mission was a failure.

There was a press conference at Sriharikota after the event. Professor Dhawan took me to the press conference. And there he announced that he took full responsibility for not achieving the mission, even though *I* was the project director and the mission director.

When we launched the SLV-3 again on 18 July 1980, we successfully placed the Rohini satellite into orbit. Again there was a press conference and this time, Professor Dhawan put me in the front to share the success story with the press.

What we learn from this event is that a true leader gives credit for success to those who worked for it, and takes responsibility for the failures of his team. That is true leadership. The scientific community in India has been fortunate to work with such leaders.

> This is an important lesson for all the young people who are aspiring to be tomorrow's leaders. The great lesson we learn here is that a leader in any field—political, administrative, scientific, education, industry, judiciary, or any other human activity—should have the capacity for creative leadership and the courage to take responsibility for failures and share successes with his team members.

Courage to Take Decisions

I still remember an incident from May 1996. It was nine o'clock at night when I got a call from the then Prime Minister P.V. Narasimha Rao's house saying that I should meet him immediately. I met him just two days before the announcement of the general election results. He told me, 'Kalam, be ready with your team for the nuclear test. I am going to Tirupati. Wait for my authorization to go ahead with the test. The DRDO-DAE teams must be ready for action.'

Of course, the election results that year were quite different from what he had anticipated. I was busy at the Chandipur missile range. I got a call saying that I must meet immediately with the prime minister designate, Atal Bihari Vajpayee, along with Narasimha Rao. I witnessed a unique situation. Shri Narasimha Rao—the outgoing prime minister—asked me to brief Vajpayeeji about the details of the nuclear programme, so that a smooth takeover of such a very important programme could take place. This incident reveals the maturity and professional excellence of a patriotic statesman who believed that the nation's cause was bigger than party politics. After taking over as prime minister in 1998, the first task Vajpayeeji gave me was to conduct the nuclear test at the earliest. Both these leaders had the courage to take difficult decisions boldly, even though the consequences of such a decision could have great national and international significance.

Nobility in Management

The next leader I would like to discuss is Professor Brahm Prakash. When I was the project director of the SLV-3 programme, Professor Brahm Prakash was the director of the Vikram Sarabhai Space Centre (VSSC), which integrated multiple institutions based on the advice of Professor Kamala Chowdhuri, a management guru from the Indian Institute of Management.

Professor Brahm Prakash took hundreds of decisions for the growth of space science and technology. One important decision, which I will always remember, was that once a programme such as the SLV-3 was sanctioned, the multiple laboratories of the VSSC as well as the multiple centres of ISRO, including the Space Department, would work to realize the stated goals of the programme *as a team*. Particularly during 1973–1980, there was a tremendous financial crunch and there were competing requirements from many small projects. He effectively converged all scientific and technological work to be focused towards SLV-3 and its satellite.

When I say that Professor Brahm Prakash is famous for the evolution of management with nobility, I would like to give a few instances. He enabled the evolution of a comprehensive management plan for the SLV-3 programme towards the mission of putting the Rohini satellite in orbit for the first time. After my task team prepared the SLV-3 management plan, he arranged nearly fifteen brainstorming meetings of the SSC (Space Scientific Committee) over a period of three months. After discussion and approval, this management plan was signed by Professor Brahm Prakash and it became the guiding spirit and the working document for the whole organization.

This was also when the national vision on space was getting converted into mission mode programmes. During the evolution of the management plan, I could see how multiple views had emerged and how many people were afraid of losing their individuality to the main mission, thereby leading to much debate and anger at the meetings. I remember how Professor Brahm Prakash presided over these meetings, with a radiant smile on his face. The anger, fear and prejudice all eventually disappeared in the presence of his thinking.

Today, the space programme, launch vehicle, spacecraft, scientific experiments and launch missions all take place in the centres of ISRO in a cohesive and cooperative manner. I learnt the hard way from him that before starting any programme, it is essential to have the project management plan, with the details of how to steer the project through different phases and how to foresee possible critical paths and possible solutions, keeping time, performance and schedule as key factors.

Working with Integrity and Succeeding with Integrity

In November 2011, I was at Jorhat, Assam, to address the World Tea Science Congress. The evening I reached, I addressed the administrative and police officers of Jorhat and Dibrugarh district in a session organized by R.C. Jain, district magistrate, Jorhat. There I administered an oath to the participants: *'I will work with integrity and succeed with integrity.'* The decibel level was very high when they said 'work with integrity' but it went down when they were repeating 'succeed with integrity'.

Creative Leadership: The Essence of Good Governance

The next day, I was at the World Tea Science Congress in the presence of the chief minister of Assam and the Jorhat adminsitrative team. There I saw a beautiful sight. The chairman of the Tea Board, M.G.V.K. Bhanu, an IAS officer, who was giving the introductory speech to the participants of the Congress said, 'Yesterday, Dr Kalam administered an oath to all the IAS and IPS officers, including myself. I would to like to assure you, Dr Kalam, that I have worked with integrity and succeeded with integrity for the past twenty-four years as an IAS officer in different parts of the state and the centre. Now I am with the Tea Board. I have also served as secretary to the CM of Assam. I would like to assure Dr Kalam that I have tried to maintain moral uprightness in all my tasks.'

Mr Bhanu also mentioned that he had been thinking about what he should be remembered for and he wanted to make India the largest producer and exporter of tea in the world.

If every functionary of the government of India has such vision and mission, I am confident that we will transform into a developed nation well before 2020.

So far, I have discussed the unique dimensions of creative leadership for governance. Here, let me recall a profound statement by Maharishi Patanjali:

> When you are inspired by some great purpose, some extraordinary project, all your thoughts break their bounds. Your mind transcends limitations, your

consciousness expands in every direction, and you find yourself in a new, great and wonderful world. Dormant forces, faculties and talents come alive, and you discover yourself to be a greater person by far than you ever dreamt yourself to be.

National Development and Creative Leadership

These are the connections between creative leadership and how it can bring about national development.

- A nation's economic development is powered by competitiveness.
- Competitiveness is powered by knowledge.
- Knowledge is powered by technology and innovation.
- Technology and innovation are powered by resource investment.
- Resource investment is powered by return on investment.
- Return on investment is powered by revenue.
- Revenue is powered by volume and repeat sales.
- Volume and repeat sales are powered by customer loyalty.
- Customer loyalty is powered by the quality and value of products.
- Quality and value of products is powered by employee productivity and innovation.
- Employee productivity is powered by employee loyalty.

- Employee loyalty is powered by employee satisfaction.
- Employee satisfaction is powered by the working environment.
- Working environment is powered by management innovation.
- Management innovation is powered by creative leadership.

For success in all national missions, it is essential to have creative leaders. Creative leadership involves exercising the vision to change the traditional role from the commander to the coach, manager to mentor, from director to delegator and from one who demands respect to one who facilitates self-respect. For enhancing enterprise value, we need a large number of creative leaders.

Vision for the Nation and Governance

When India transforms into an economically developed nation, our citizens can live in a green clean environment without pollution, have prosperity and peace. I am sure that the qualities of creative leadership discussed here will lay the foundations for the transformation of India.

Inclusive Growth for Good Governance

Right to aspire for dignity and distinction is the prerogative of every citizen in a democracy.

Gaps in Our Growth

I feel that the core competence of our nation is its ability to manage a multi-lingual, multi-religious and multi-cultural society of over a billion people within a democratic set-up. In the last sixty-four years, we have demonstrated our strengths as the largest democracy in the world. Of course, we have several areas we need to improve upon in order to achieve our goal of a developed India by the year 2020.

We are a country of diversity. We have some of the richest people in the world on one hand and 270 million people living below the poverty line on the other. We have realized the Mars Orbiter Mission on one hand, but on the other, we are yet to make everyone literate in our country. We have had outstanding Indian women showcasing their capabilities in many fields around the world while at the same time, violence against women in our country continues to grow. We have several hundred aeroplanes ferrying millions across metropolitan cities; at the same time, we still have villages that are yet to be connected by roads.

So the priority of our country should be inclusive growth and how to bring it about. For realizing this, we have to strengthen the multiple organs of governance: our legislature, our executive, our judiciary and our media should be transformed.

In my view, the fundamental building block in this whole process is the enlightened human being—he or she could be a people's representative, an administrator, a judge, a media person or one belonging to any other profession. But what do I mean by the term 'enlightened human being'? Let me start with some recent experiences to illustrate this.

Traits of an Enlightened Human Being

> Good governance is, in the end, carried out by individuals and teams. The quality of people who provide governance decides the success or failure of schemes. Good people lead to positive results in governance.

I have mentioned earlier how I witnessed the 100th birthday

celebrations of Sree Sree Sivakumara Swamiji of Siddaganga Math in Tumkur. In April 2009, I was invited back for his 102nd year celebrations, where he spoke to the large gathering and I listened to his words, mesmerized. He said that for a happy and peaceful society, each citizen has to develop two traits: one is intellect and the other humaneness. These can be acquired through good parenting, good teachers, good books and by being in the company of great people. If this is not done at the right age, human beings can become like the devil, particularly if the intellect acts without humaneness. I feel we, as a nation, have to take this message from Swamiji and develop these traits in the youth of the country.

Here, I am reminded of the story of Imam Ghazali as another example of a good human being. This incident was narrated to me by my father.

Imam Ghazali was a saint teacher who lived in the twelfth century. One day, Imam Ghazali was unfolding his prayer mat for Maghrib namaz. Shaitan, the angel who transgressed, appeared in front of him in order to test him and said, 'Respected Imam Sahib, I am coming from heaven right now, where there was a discussion about great human beings. You have been judged as the best human being on earth. As recognition of your great stature, you have been exempted from the trouble of performing namaz in the future.'

Imam Ghazali was restless since the time for namaz was approaching. So he looked at Shaitan and said, 'Shaitan Sahib, first of all, performing namaz is no trouble at all and when even Prophet Mohammed (peace be upon him) was not exempted from performing namaz five times a day, how can a poor imam like me not do so?' Saying this, he went on to perform the namaz. When he was done, Imam Ghazali saw that Shaitan was still standing there. Imam sahib asked him what he was waiting for. Shaitan said, 'O Imam, you have excelled even the most favoured Prophet Adam, who could not win against my deception and I made him eat the forbidden fruit.' Realizing that Shaitan was flattering him, Imam sahib prayed to Allah, 'Oh Almighty, help me and save me from the deception of flattery,' thus making the disappointed Shaitan finally disappear.

Friends, what is the message from the incidents that I have recounted? Not only do we have to develop intellect and humaneness, but also guard against temptations in order to succeed in our mission of human welfare.

The India We Aspire For

Let me put forward my visualization of India by the year 2020.

We want to create a nation where the rural and urban divide is minimal; where there is an equitable distribution of natural resources; where various sectors of the economy show consistent growth; where value-based education is available to all; where learned people receive recognition; where healthcare is available to all; where poverty is eradicated; where governance is without corruption; where women receive equal opportunities in every stage of life and finally, a nation that is safe from strife.

Integrated Action for Developed India

To achieve this profile of India, we need to develop sectors like Agriculture, Education, Healthcare, Information and Communication Technology and Infrastructure in all parts of the country in a coordinated and integrated manner.

For the last few decades, we have heard a statement being repeated quite often by responsible leaders: 'From the amount allotted for the development programmes for the people, not even ten per cent reaches the targeted people.' Therein lies the question: why not? Every one of us needs to apply our mind to overcome this situation.

This can only be done through value-based education and by building leadership at all levels. Leaders need to be educated, they need to be prepared for decision making, envisioning, planning and then implementing programmes, and they also need to know how to manage failures.

Traits of Leadership

As I have said, I have seen three dreams which have taken shape through vision, mission and realization: the space programme of ISRO, the AGNI programme of DRDO and PURA (Providing

Urban Amenities to Rural Areas). Of course, these three programmes succeeded in the midst of many challenges and problems. I have worked in all three areas and I want to convey to you what I have learnt about leadership from these programmes:

- A leader must have a vision.
- A leader must have the passion to realize the vision.
- A leader must be able to travel on an unexplored path.
- A leader must know how to manage both success and failure.
- A leader must have the courage to take decisions.
- A leader should have nobility in management.
- A leader should be transparent in every action.
- A leader must work with integrity and succeed with integrity.

For strengthening the institution of governance in the country, we have to generate creative leaders through the nurturing of talent and the promotion of innovation in every sphere of national activity.

For enhancing the performance of our elected MPs in coordination with the panchayats and the district magistrates of the district, I have suggested that it is essential to bring out a database of six main points for each one of the 543 constituencies, which will provide guidelines to the elected members on what they need to look into after the elections. Members of various political parties and the media can generate the data in a month's time. The district magistrates, in fact, should have enough powers of execution so that they can function as CEOs of the districts, assuming responsibilities and delivering good governance to the people as his or her core job description.

Constituency Database

- The present per-capita income of all the citizens;
- Data on the literacy level of the people;
- Data on all the water bodies and their status with respect to desilting and interconnection of inlets and outlets;
- The core competence and resources of the villages, which will enable the taking up of rural development projects and provide value-added employment to all the citizens of the villages;
- The present IMR (Infant Mortality Rate) and MMR (Maternal Mortality Rate) of all villages;
- The availability of safe drinking water and electricity to all families in the villages.

This database could become the basis for planning and action of all the developmental tasks of the district, as soon as the MPs are elected with a five-year target in front of them. The types of performance that I have suggested are:

Inclusive Growth for Good Governance

- Improving the per-capita income of the constituency by three times;
- Increasing literacy by at least 20 per cent with respect to the male and 30 per cent with respect to the female population;
- Making all the water bodies desilted and interconnected;
- Reducing the IMR and MMR to less than 10 per 1000;
- Generating value-added employment opportunities to all rural citizens;
- Providing safe drinking water;
- Providing electricity for every home.

Rule of Law

All of us, irrespective of the segment of the system to which we belong, have to regulate ourselves by a code of behaviour as ordained by the Constitution, tacitly or otherwise. Freedom available to a segment, who are elected by a majority of the voting citizens, is to be used for the formulation of wholesome legalistic stipulations within the framework of the Constitution for common good and not for imprudent enactments that only have transient appeal to one particular section or another. Likewise, discreteness is a virtue to be cultivated and exercised. Actions once taken cannot be undone. If one of the organs of the system arranges a midnight rendezvous compromising the rule of law by entering into concessions with outlaws, it is not exactly getting swathed in glory. The rule of law is compromised and the whole system receives a body blow.

Independence of jurisdiction does not mean licence to override good sense. Friends, I am voicing my concern, as a citizen of this country, about the denial of the rule of law implicitly, yet unmistakably, promised to the citizen by the Constitution of India.

> Privileges are meant to be enjoyed with prudence by those on whom they are conferred; they are not meant to make others suffer and certainly they are not meant to be flaunted. Rights are meant to be exercised for achieving the right thing; they are not to be brandished. Politeness and moderation are virtues to be cultivated and self-restraint by each of the organs of the system, coupled with respect for others, should be consciously remembered and conscientiously followed with unflinching loyalty, sincerity and honesty. The earlier the realization comes to each of the pillars of democracy, namely the legislature, executive and judiciary, that one cannot live without the other two for a healthy and dynamic democratic system, the better for all of us.

We should strive to see real democracy blossom forth into a system that allows free flow of the citizen's genuine aspirations.

The system should facilitate every individual to not only express but also develop themselves further without treading on one another's feet. Such realization would automatically lead to self-discipline and that would be the best prescription for a healthy and resurgent democratic system.

Indian democracy faces many challenges, but we need to see these challenges as great opportunities. Our successful experiments to improve the condition of one-sixth of the world's population will provide lessons for the entire human race.

E-governance for Transparent Societies

Connectivity empowers.

Good governance is being recognized as an important goal by countries across the world. Several nations have taken up specific initiatives for open government. Freedom of information is being redefined and supported by detailed guidelines. In this context, the Internet revolution has proved to be a powerful tool for good governance initiatives. The Internet enables the availability of services any time, anywhere, a real possibility.

Along with this there is also a conscious effort to put the citizen as the point of focus in governance. Citizens are being perceived as customers and the delivery of services to citizens is now being considered a primary function of the government.

In a democratic nation of over a billion people such as India, e-governance will enable seamless access to information and, in a federal set-up such as ours, ensure the flow of information from the state to the centre and vice versa.

Trust and Confidence in Governance

As a function of governance, the government needs to provide multiple facilities and services to its people. These services also require to be constantly upgraded with the use of technology for fulfilling the changing needs and aspirations of the people. The government budgets and expends a large amount of funds for fulfilling this goal. In its Five Year Plans, it allocates a million crore for national development. The money for this work comes from the people, through taxes, to be spent for the benefit of all people, particularly the needy.

However, when it comes to the benefits reaching the common man, the value of the services that reaches the citizen is much below expectations. This happens in all service sectors, namely education, healthcare, sanitation, water, power, infrastructure tele-communication as well as in many other areas of importance such as the seeking of loans from banks for agriculture and small-scale industries. Citizens even have to struggle for the timely payment of certain services and sometimes have to adopt wrong means for making the payment.

> The government is responsible for the betterment of the lives of the people by enacting appropriate policies and laws and by facilitating societal transformation. The success of the policies the government enacts varies with the management style adopted by it. Our

people have shown enormous resilience and have achieved phenomenal success when provided with an environment of trust and confidence. Whenever there has been a programme run on mission mode, through a specially conceived management structure, we have seen very satisfactory results, whether in governmental, quasi-governmental or private sectors.

The Concept of E-governance

I visualize e-governance as this:

> A transparent, smart system of governance with seamless access and secure and authentic flow of information that crosses inter-departmental barriers and provides fair and unbiased service to the citizens.

I have always been an advocate of using technology for the betterment of our society. E-governance is one such opportunity. But I would like all of you to remember that technology is a double-edged sword. If we don't have an implementation plan from concept to completion, technology becomes expensive and we are not able to properly reap the benefits. Hence, it is essential for the nation to implement the e-governance process fast. While doing this, we must also have a quantitative measure of the impact of e-governance on our society. Every year, we must be able to measure the number of people who have been touched by the benefits of e-governance.

Benefits of Computerization

Perhaps many of my younger readers do not even remember the manner in which we had to make train, bus and air ticket reservations a few decades ago. We had to stand in long queues a couple of months before the date of travel (for train tickets) or visit the airline office and bus stations. Now, with the advent of Internet and mobile-based reservation systems, we are able to get this work done with minimum wastage of time. Transactions are clean and hassle-free and we can do this while on the move as well.

Similarly, the benefits of Internet-based payment of telephone and electricity bills implemented by many telephone and electricity boards have led to ease for customers. Our voters' cards are now made available to us by applying through forms that can be downloaded from the Election Commission's websites and by following the instructions available on the site.

All of these are examples of ways in which people are not only able to complete tasks with ease, but also do so without involving middlemen, thereby reducing the avenues for harassment and corruption.

Transparency in E-governance

Today's information technology and communication systems have ended all concerns of time and distance. There is a new paradigm in this system of democratization of information: one where information can be accessed at any time from anywhere in the world.

India needs to transform into a transparent society, and for that, it is essential that government functions which have public interface or interactions—especially where the state and central functionaries have to provide correct information—be done through the tools of information technology and communication. This means that software has to be written to codify the rules and procedures of government functions, which the public can then access. Then only can we provide equal access to all, and exceptions to the rule can be made in a transparent manner.

Since India's core competence is in information technology and communication, transparency in administration and management through e-commerce and e-business, leading to e-governance, is definitely possible. Actions have to be initiated in mission mode. An appropriate legal system should also be in place to validate such modes of interaction.

Some Visible Good Governance Practices

Now I would like to discuss some of the visible practices of good and transparent governance as practised by the three pillars of our democracy.

Legislative System: The passing of the Right to Education Act 2009, the Right to Information Act 2005, and the National Rural Employment Guarantee Act 2005 are some examples of the effective functioning of the legislative system. These Acts are structured to fulfill a part of the aspirations of our citizens.

Executive System: Some of the key accomplishments of the executive system have been the time-bound realization of the metro railway system in Delhi; the successful, though partial, implementation of e-governance models in certain states, bringing about substantial transparency in the system; a working model of the railway reservation system; the virtual university initiatives by three 150-year-old universities of the country, namely Madras, Calcutta and Mumbai; and the healthcare services provided through the Yeshaswini scheme. Innovative monitoring systems for electrical energy generation and distribution, leading to the reduction of losses and pilferage, have made a few state electricity boards profitable institutions.

Judicial System: Delay in justice also adds to corruption. I am extremely happy to see that our judicial system has risen to take on this challenge well. I was also very happy to see certain cases where justice was administered speedily. These are good models to emulate for a speedy justice delivery system. However, there are millions of cases pending in different courts for justice. An e-governance judicial system should enable categorization and priority allocation for the speedy disposal of cases.

The judgements of the Supreme Court and some High Courts are now available on the Internet. This step has considerably relieved the agony of the litigants and also enables others to use these judgements in their areas of interest. This is a giant step towards transparency. It is essential that all other courts in the country also follow this model. They need to be facilitated by the Law ministry, the state governments and the higher judiciary in these endeavours. In addition to this, landmark directions from the Supreme Court on the use of CNG, and the interlinking of rivers will also have a large impact on the welfare of the society.

Litigation free villages: I would like to recall one of my experiences when I was in Chitrakoot, Madhya Pradesh, some years ago. I met a great man, of whom many of you might have heard about. He is the famous ninety-year-old social activist, Dr (Nanaji) Deshmukh. He was instrumental in making eighty villages 'litigation free' through the DRI (Deendayal Research Institute). This was a successful experiment for resolving disputes within families and within villages. Nanaji said he aimed to create a beautiful society, an empowered society and, above all, a society with moral values.

So it is possible to create a corruption-free society by enlisting good human beings, and spreading the message of their success.

Some National Challenges

One of our nation's biggest challenges is the upliftment of the 270 million people who are below the poverty line. They need housing, food, healthcare, and they need education and employment, which will enable them to lead a good life. Our GDP is oscillating between 4-6 per cent per annum, whereas economists suggest that to uplift the people below poverty line, our economy has to grow at the rate of 10 per cent per annum consistently for over a decade.

Integrated Action for Development

To meet the needs of over one billion people, our primary mission should be to transform India into a developed nation. There are five areas where India has core competencies for integrated action: (1) Agriculture and Food Processing (2) Reliable and Quality Electric Power, Surface Transport and Infrastructure for all parts of the country (3) Education and Healthcare (4) Information and Communication Technology (5) Strategic Sectors. These five areas are closely inter-related and when effectively addressed, would lead to food, economic, energy and national security.

To implement programmes in an integrated way as well as in a time-bound and cost-effective fashion in order to provide necessary services to the citizens equitably and with ease, it is essential that we use the technology available to us today and work out a comprehensive e-governance system for all government to government and government to citizens transactions.

No country has so far implemented an e-governance system for over one billion people. Therefore, it is a big challenge for us.

The Ideal Scenario

As an example of the use of technology in the democratic process, I visualize an election scenario where a candidate files his nomination from a particular constituency. Immediately, the election officer verifies the authenticity from the national citizen ID database through a multipurpose citizen ID card. The candidate's civic consciousness and citizenship behaviour can also be accessed through the police crime record. The property records come from the land registration authority across the country. Income and wealth resources come from the income tax department, as well as other sources. The person's education credentials come from his university records. The track record of employment comes from various employers with whom he has worked. The credit history comes from various credit institutions like banks. The person's legal track records come from the judicial system.

All the details arrive at the computer terminal of the election officer within a few minutes through the e-governance software, which tracks various state and central government web services directories through the network, collects the information quickly and automatically and presents facts in real-time without any bias.

An artificial intelligence software would analyse the candidate's credentials and give a rating on how successful that person would be as a politician. The election officer can then make an informed choice and start the electoral processes.

Is this a dream? Is this possible? If possible, by when can we implement it? Can we provide good governance to over one billion people? Can e-governance speed up the delivery system? Can e-governance differentiate between genuine transactions and spurious ones? Can e-governance ensure immediate action for genuine cases and stop action on spurious transactions? Can this be done at a cost affordable by our nation?

Challenges of E-governance

I will now try to seek an answer for the questions I asked by asking another set of questions. Do we have the framework required for e-governance? Do we have a national citizen database that will be the primary source of information for all governance across state and central governments? Do we have standards for the exchange of secure information with non-repudiation across state and central government departments seamlessly? Do we have a secure delivery framework, that is, a virtual private network that connects state and central government departments across the country? Do we have data centres in central and state governments to handle the departmental workflow automation, collaboration, interaction, and the exchange of information with authentication? Should our administrative systems be empowered and reformed so that they can accelerate decision-making processes? When will the entire administrative body be able to contribute more towards national development rather than entangling itself in bureaucratic processes?

Let us try to find an answer to each of the above questions by asking ourselves: How can we evolve such a system? Let me focus on the Societal Grid model proposed by me to ensure overall inclusive development by connecting the various domains that will make a visible impact on the quality of life of the people.

Connectivity Model: Societal Grid

In the proposed model, the Knowledge Grid, the Rural (PURA) Grid, the Health Grid and the Governance Grid is a system of multiple portals. This system of Grids will bring prosperity to about 843 million people in the rural areas and about 343 million people in the urban areas. In the process, it will ensure that the lives of the people below the poverty line are transformed.

First let me talk about the Knowledge Grid. For bridging the rural and urban divide and ensuring the equitable distribution of prosperity, India needs to be connected. The core of this connectivity model is the partnership between governmental and other institutions both in public and private domains. The strength of this partnership is facilitated by the free flow of knowledge and information.

The Knowledge Grid

The endeavour here is to transform an information society into a knowledge society. The knowledge society will be a society producing, marketing and using products and services that are rich in both explicit and tacit knowledge, thus creating value-added products for national and international consumption. In the knowledge economy, the objective of a society changes from merely fulfilling the basic needs of all-round development to *empowerment*. For instance, the education system, instead of going by textbook teaching, will promote creative and interactive self-learning—both formal and informal—with a focus on values, merit and quality. Workers, instead of being skilled or semi-skilled, will be knowledgeable, self-empowered and flexibly skilled. Types of work, instead of being structured and hardware driven, will be more flexible and software driven. Management styles will be delegative rather than directive. In this model, the impact on environment and ecology will also be strikingly less compared to the industrial economy model. The economy itself will be knowledge driven. The key infrastructure required for this is telecom and all related tools of communication such as computers and software.

In this model, it is essential to provide equitable access to an education system that moves beyond the classroom. The bandwidth is a demolisher of imbalances and a great leveller in a knowledge society. We have rich knowledge institutions but what we need is connectivity. This connectivity is technologically possible today but would require the creation of a reliable network infrastructure, with a high bandwith of at least 10 Gigabits per second, all through the country, to provide uniform access of knowledge in different regions, leading to the creation of the Knowledge Grid.

Inter-connecting Universities with Socio-economic Institutions, Industries and R&D Organizations

India is planning to connect 5,000 institutions across the country with a Gigabit network for the creation of a collaborative knowledge-sharing platform. Three of India's 150-year-old universities, namely, the University of Madras, the University of Calcutta and the University of Mumbai, have created a 'Virtual University' to provide ten unique joint post-graduate programmes to students of these three universities thus providing quality education without regional affiliations. India has also embarked upon the mission of providing quality education services to fifty-three African nations by connecting its seven universities.

The Healthcare Grid

This is based on inter-connecting the healthcare institutions of the government, corporate and super speciality hospitals, as well as research institutions, educational institutions and ultimately, pharma R&D institutions. India has connected around 300 remote locations so far, with more than forty-five super speciality hospitals, and provides tele-medicine connectivity. In addition, programmes for providing healthcare services to fifty-three African nations by connecting twelve super speciality hospitals from India as a part of the Pan African e-Network is in progress.

Healthcare training institutes, which include nurses, paramedical staff and doctors, and medical research institutions, should also be added to the Healthcare Grid. This will enable unique case studies and experiences to be exchanged between healthcare institutions. It will also be possible to conduct conferences where specialist doctors from various remote centres can discuss critical disease patterns and provide treatment.

The E-governance Grid

Inter-connecting the central and state governments as well as district and block level offices for G2G and G2C connectivity is a part of the E-governance Grid. India is creating State Wide Area Network (SWAN) across the country and has fibre connectivity up to the block level.

The PURA Knowledge Grid

This Grid is the backbone for rural development. All other Grids will infuse knowledge into this Grid for sustainable development, healthcare and good governance. Through the PURA Grid, integrated Common Service Centres will act as an interconnected delivery mechanism for tele-education, tele-medicine and e-governance services besides individual access by people within and between village knowledge centres.

Village Knowledge Centres

For providing knowledge connectivity to the PURA Grid, village knowledge centres will act as the front-line delivery system. I visualize the establishment of village knowledge centres in village panchayats to empower villagers with knowledge and to act as a local centre for knowledge connectivity within the overall framework of PURA. The village knowledge centre should provide essential data required for targeted populations, such as farmers, fishermen, craftsmen, traders, businessmen, entrepreneurs, unemployed youths and students. One million Common Service Centres (CSCs) have been set up across the country through public-private partnership to address these issues.

The main focus of the CSC is to not only provide information and e-governance but also to empower the youth to undertake development tasks in the villages and establish rural enterprises, which, in turn, will lead to large scale rural employment. So, it is essential to skill-enable and knowledge-enable with the help of academic institutions, industry, banking and marketing institutions. The CSC should act as a facilitator.

PURA Nodal Knowledge Data Centre

Kisan Call Centres provide valuable and timely knowledge support to farmers and fishermen. Similar domain service provider call centres are required in the field of commerce and industry, entrepreneurial skill development and employment generation, travel and tourism, banking and insurance, meteorological forecasting, disaster warning systems, education and human resource development and healthcare.

These call centres will act as service providers to the PURA Nodal Knowledge Data Centres located in the PURA complexes, which, in turn, will provide area specific and customized knowledge to the village knowledge centres (or CSCs) in the villages in a holistic manner. This delivery will depend on the availability of robust connectivity in different parts of the country. The PURA Grid, then, will draw information from the other Grids and will act as a catalyst for societal transformation in rural areas.

The Right to Information in Governance

*Right information enriches knowledge,
knowledge makes the nation great.*

The Right to Information Act has been in operation since 2005. I am sure a number of citizens have benefitted from seeking information on various aspects of the government. Sometimes, the information sought leads to suggestions for improving the functioning of certain institutions, provided the information has been sought properly and the provided information has been understood by the receiver. However, to derive maximum benefit from this Act, active participation of all stakeholders—political leaders, people in the civil services and the media, societal transformers and citizens—is required. This will also make India a highly participative democracy.

The country is also poised to implement e-governance at all levels, which, like the RTI, will bring further transparence in the processes of governance.

How do we provide good governance to over one billion people? Can e-governance speed up the delivery of the results of sound policy to the people? E-governance and access to information are a means to an end. We need enlightened citizens to realize the full benefits of the governance systems, because, ultimately, it is the people who uphold ethics, morality and righteousness.

National E-governance Programme and RTI

The NeGEP (National E-governance Programme) was set up for implementing government to citizen services and for establishing the State Wide Area Network (SWAN) with State Data Centres, with 2 mbps connectivity up to the block level and with 100,000 CSCs at the front end. The primary focus of the NeGEP is to upgrade the quality of governance by vastly improving the delivery of government services. It is essential to establish the G2G E-governance Grid by connecting District Level Data Centres to a State Data Centre. The G2G E-governance Grid enables secured dynamic work flow across government units thus ensuring the seamless flow of files.

In the name of security, we shouldn't delay the implementation of the e-governance system any further. In the digital environment, security implementation is highly important. If a secure IT environment is in place, all actions and transactions are traceable at all levels through system-oriented and application-oriented audit trails, making it very difficult for anyone to remove their digital footprints, leading to transparency in governance. In fact, it is in the present manual system that security is much more vulnerable.

Hence, a secure G2G E-governance Grid will serve as the backbone of the e-governance system right from the highest echelons of the state and central government to district level and block level administration. If this connectivity is established truly and properly, then access to the Right to Information Act, right from the bottom of the e-governance pyramid to the top, will be ensured. Establishing the G2G E-governance Grid is vital for the effective implementation of the RTI Act.

Checks and Balances to the RTI

As the largest democratic nation in the world, India has survived all kinds of vicissitudes and turbulences over the last half century and more. Our democratic system has been gaining from strength to strength, although there have also been weaknesses in the system. Our strength has always lain in overcoming those weaknesses and setting ourselves firmly on the road to higher and higher levels of democratic efficiency and progress.

In this context, the RTI has been an important milestone. The Act assures every citizen the right to know what the citizen should, and throws open the system of governance to total transparency and therefore, inescapable accountability. Adequate safeguards have been built into the Act to ensure that the right is exercised in accordance with the dictates of national security, which, of course, cannot be compromised under any circumstances. After all, every right has to have checks built in to prevent its unbridled use.

Grievance Removal Through Information

I am reminded of a case which happened in 2004. On 26 May 2004, when the CBSE announced the twelfth standard results for Uttar Pradesh, one student's world collapsed. This student, who had consistently scored grades in the 90s, had been awarded very low marks only in one subject. A request to look into the matter came to me when I was the President. On examining the merits of the case, I directed that the matter be looked into by the education board. This was done and the discrepancy was sorted out. Of course, after this incident I was flooded with emails with similar requests most of which were not genuine. The point I am making here is not so much the fact that the problem was solved for this particular case, but the need for an online system where corrective action can take place without the need for individuals to go to the apex of the system.

Organizations can take various proactive steps to assess the frequently asked information by citizens and make sure these are available for the public.

Assessment of Information Needs

Every public authority should continuously assess the information needs of the people who contact them from time to time. This will help the authority concerned to ascertain what kind of information is generally requested for by the people. All such information that has been requested for a number of times or by more than one citizen should be uploaded on that public authority's website and updated from time to time. This will save time and resources and will also diminish the chances of any divergent interpretation by the person seeking information. The best way to avoid such an event is to make available as much information as possible by the public authority itself. When information is available in the public domain for ready access, the possibility of its misuse or misinterpretation diminishes. Websites such as these should be updated weekly so that the most recent and most relevant information is available to those seeking it.

When the government accepts and acts upon suggestions made to it by bodies like the Comptroller and Auditor General then these actions should also be mentioned on the website.

Governmental authorities have to ensure that the applicant

does not use the information for purposes other than the intended purpose stated in the Act. The seeking of information should always be in public interest and for public good, which is the essence of freedom of information.

Implementing the Fundamental Right of the Citizen

The Constitution of India has declared that the fundamental right to speech and expression and the fundamental right to life and liberty should also include the right of the citizen to access information. Every public authority must try to implement the provisions of the Right to Information Act under this spirit of implementing the fundamental right of the citizen.

Rashtrapati Bhavan Experience

I am told that 99 per cent of the applications coming to the Rashtrapati Bhavan Secretariat are on matters unrelated to the Rashtrapati Bhavan. Due to lack of awareness, these applications are sent here since people, it seems, believe that the President of India is directly responsible for and can rectify their complaints—everything from issues related to departmental promotions to land disputes. Sometimes, despite knowing that the President is not directly responsible, people write to the Rashtrapati Bhavan as a last resort. These applications are transferred to the concerned departments for action.

This may also be the situation with government departments. This lack of awareness in the public leads to delays for them and also places a heavy burden on the working of the departments. I would suggest that the CIC (Central Information Commission) evolve guidelines and provide it to the seekers of information about where and how to get the required information. Simultaneously, the information should be put up on the website so that same questions are not repeatedly asked.

I would like to suggest that the Commission run extensive publicity campaigns to inform the citizen about who deals with what in the Indian federal set-up. The Commission could also find out how many applications are received by various departments and ministries which have to be transferred and how much time is lost in doing so.

Also, the website of the Commission (www.cic.gov.in) should have a search engine, where CPIOs (Central Public Information Officers) can quickly look up decisions of the Commission on cases which have come up before them. At present, the Commission's website has a section called 'Decisions of CIC', which gives the text of the decisions arrived at in cases which have come to them for appeal. The text is a scanned image and the decisions are stored quarter-wise and therefore, if a CPIO wants to consult a case decision, it is a time-consuming process since he/she has to go through every case decision to find the one that has a reference to the point of law which is sought. A search engine will be able to drastically reduce the time consumed in these processes.

Transparency is the basis of good governance, and a clean conscience is the basis of transparency. Once the conscience is clear, there can be no difficulty in making one's actions an open book. Similarly, in a government, making information available to all the stakeholders of the system is not only commendable but essential for the better functioning of the state.

The Effects of Corruption

*Righteousness in the heart
leads to order in the nation.*

Certain Experiences in Governance

It is well known that in government schemes and welfare projects, sometimes there is fictitious reporting or the full money allotted is shown as spent and claims of objectives being fully met are not backed up by proper evidence to corroborate the claims.

Thus we can see that in the absence of a non-transparent system, a well-intentioned programme fails to produce the desired results. This clearly shows the effect of corruption on governance and the failure of our system to protect the human rights of citizens.

Studies show that the levels of corruption vary from state to state. The reasons for this should be established. Can it be due to political awareness? Can it be due to better Human Development Index? Can it be due to an alert media? Can it be due to women's empowerment? It may be useful to study these aspects and assess the possible reasons, so that they can be emulated by other states.

Identifying the Heroes

In any village or panchayat or district, we will always find at least a few corruption-free good human beings. We may even find pockets of corruption-free societies. If these can be identified and celebrated, we can create a nearly corruption-free state. The real-world examples of corruption-free individuals and groups and societies must be discussed publicly, so that they can become examples to be followed in the country. A nation can be corruption free only when its states are corruption free; a state can be corruption free only if its districts are corruption free; a district can be corruption free only if its panchayats are corruption free; a panchayat can be corruption free only if the people are corruption free; and people can be corruption free only if they have imbibed these values from their childhood.

Certain Experiences in Societal Life

The creation of a corruption-free society depends heavily on the environment at home, the school, the society and the government, besides on the individual. Let me discuss the various components of this complex fabric.

Corruption-Free Society Starts at Home

On 21 November 2005, I visited Adichunchanagiri Math to attend a function of the Foundation for Unity of Religions and Enlightened Citizenship. I interacted with over 54,000 students of various schools and colleges of Karnataka. There, a tenth-standard student, M. Bhavani, studying at Adichunchanagiri Composite High School, Shimoga, asked me the following question: 'Sir, I would like to be a citizen of a corruption-free nation. Please tell me, as a student, how can I contribute?'

The agony of a young mind is reflected in this question. For me, it was an important question, since it came from a young person. As I thought about what answer I could give her, my thoughts were as follows:

There are over a billion people in the country and nearly 200 million homes. In general, there are good citizens everywhere. However, if we find that the people in a few million houses are not transparent and not amenable to the laws of the country, what can we do? This is where young people come in: they are the ones who can eradicate corruption from its base, that is, the home. If the parents in these houses are deviating from the honest path then the children need to guide their parents or their elders on to the right path with love, affection and encouragement.

I told all the children assembled at that gathering that in case their parents were deviating from the path of transparency and honesty, they needed to speak up and boldly take their parents to task, reminding them that they taught their children right from wrong, and were, therefore, setting a bad example. Most of the children spontaneously responded, 'We will do it.'

Similarly, I have also told parents the same thing in another meeting. Initially there was silence, but later, many of them hesitantly agreed that they would abide by the children's suggestion since it was driven by love. They took an oath in front of me. It was: 'I will lead an honest life free from all corruption and will set an example for others to adopt a transparent way of life.'

Finally I told the students that they should start a movement against corruption that begins at their home. I am confident that children can reform their families.

The Mission of the Teacher

School is the next important environment where character is shaped. The prime learning period for children is between five to seventeen years of age. Through the learning years, the student spends approximately 25,000 hours at the school campus. Hence school hours are the best time for learning, making it crucial that the school has the best of environment: mission-oriented learning with a value system in place. As Bestolozzy, a Greek teacher said, *Give me a child for seven years. Afterwards, let the God or the devil take the child. They cannot change the child.*

That is the great confidence of the teacher. What a mission for teachers to build character and inculcate high morals in the students of the country!

Elevating Young Minds

The next component I would like to discuss is the importance of moral classes for students in order to elevate their minds. While I was in college, I remember the lectures given by the highest authority of the Jesuit institution, Rev Father Rector Kalathil of St Joseph's College, Tiruchirapalli. Every Monday, he would take an hour-long class. He talked about good human beings of the present and the past, and what creates goodness in human beings. In this class, he would give lectures on personalities such as the Buddha, Confucius, St Augustine, Khalifa Omar, Mahatma Gandhi, Einstein, Abraham Lincoln and several others as well as moral stories linked to our civilizational heritage. He also talked about great personalities who had made huge contributions towards the service of the people.

It is essential in secondary schools and colleges to arrange for lectures by great teachers once a week on such topics. This will elevate young minds and teach them to love their country, to love other human beings and inculcate noble values in them.

Code of Conduct

The fourth important component for promoting a transparent society is forming an informal code of conduct for people in high places of responsibility. Here I am reminded of a line from a Tamil classic, which brings out the power of righteousness and provides a code of conduct for the people in high and responsible positions.

It says that if people who are in high and responsible positions go against righteousness, righteousness itself will be transformed into a destroyer. Whoever deviates from righteousness, whether they are the individual or the state, is responsible for their own actions. This message is mentioned very clearly by Ilango Adigal in *Silappathikaram*, one of the five great Tamil epics written nearly 2,000 years ago.

So far, I have been talking about the strategies needed for the creation of enlightened citizens. Now I would like to discuss transparency in governance, which is one of the primary requirements of the democratic system.

Trust and Confidence in Governance

We have to imagine a scene. I call it 'A Scene of Sweat'. It is the farmer in the agricultural field, the fisherman in the rough sea, the worker in the factory, the teacher in the school, the knowledge worker in the laboratory, the health worker in healthcare institutions and many, many others who have to be remembered when we take a political, administrative or judicial decision. I would consider a government machinery corruption free only if the purpose for which the machinery has been set up is fulfilled, in letter and in spirit, with honesty, sincerity and purposefulness.

How to Create a Corruption-free Society

Some of the methodologies here would be the introduction of a robust system of e-governance. I have discussed this in detail in my essay, 'E-governance for Transparent Societies'.

E-governance has already shown its impact in our legislative, executive and judicial systems. In the legislative system, the Right to Education Act 2009, the Right to Information Act 2005, and the National Rural Employment Guarantee Act 2005 are some of the recent examples of the effective functioning of the legislative system. In the executive system, we have implemented partial e-governance in certain states, including a working railway reservation system, and the creation of a virtual university through the combined efforts of three universities of the country. In the judiciary, implementation of e-governance has led to the speedy resolution of several cases. The judgements of the Supreme Court and some High Courts are now available on the Internet.

> A corruption-free society is not merely a dream, it is entirely achievable. All we need is the role of the enlightened citizen in the creation of a method of governance that promotes transparency and honesty for the better functioning of democracy.

Conscience is the light of the soul. It raises its voice in protest whenever anything that is contrary to truth and righteousness is thought of or done. Conscience is a form of truth that has been transferred through our genetic stock in the form of knowledge of our own acts and knowing right from wrong. Only a virtuous and courageous person can use the instrument of conscience and that person alone can clearly hear the inner voice of the soul. In a wicked person, this faculty is dead. The sensitive nature of the conscience gets destroyed by sin or corruption and the person is unable to discriminate right from wrong. Those who are leading organizations, business enterprises, institutions and governments should develop this virtue: the ability to use their own conscience.

In this connection, I would like to recall a hymn that I heard at a spiritual centre.

Where there is righteousness in the heart,
There is beauty in the character.
When there is beauty in the character,
There is harmony in the home.
When there is harmony in the home,
There is order in the nation.
When there is order in the nation,
There is peace in the world.

It reflects the beautiful connectivity between heart, character, home, nation and the world. In a society, we need to build righteousness among all its constituents. For the society as a whole to be righteous, we need to inculcate values of righteousness in the family, in education, service, career, business and industry, civil administration, politics, government, law and order and righteousness in justice.

Public Audit and Good Governance

*Public audit is a partner in the
mission of national development.*

While addressing an annual convention of auditors general, I had spoken about the need for timely feedback from auditors on government projects. This results in transparency as well as smooth running of any mission.

Importance of Public Audits

The CAG (Comptroller and Auditor General) has been continuously improving the audit system and they have brought in the concept of the performance audit, which has added value to our system. The study of the significance of developmental programmes, the pointing out of deviation, the investigation of their causes and the suggestion of better practices have improved the performance of certain systems. Today, the audit goes beyond mere economic aspects and evaluates the efficiency and effectiveness of government programmes. Also, since 2000, the CAG has reached out to major development initiatives of the government in areas of health, education, urban employment generation, rural employment generation, food security, basic infrastructure creation and accelerated irrigation benefit programmes. Thus, I can see the audit becoming a partner in national development.

I am aware that whenever an audit report is done—which is then transformed into an audit para and then a few result in oral evidence by the PAC (Public Accounts Committee)—a lot of hue and cry emanates about all the details not having been looked at. Sometimes it is due to political motivations. That is why I normally suggest that there should be system audit and not a part audit. A certain amount of criticism will always be there when problems in the organization are pointed out. But if the conclusions are built on sound arguments through established facts, and the results are going to assist the organization, the auditors should remain undeterred.

Closed Loop Guidance and Control

Let me give you an event-based experience of the missile programme, which has some similarity to the mission of the CAG. When I see the audit and corrective action needed in the financial management field, I am reminded of technical events taking place in sequence in the case of a flight trajectory. Let me refer to the launch of the AGNI missile system. It is a controlled and guided flight from the time of launch till it reaches the target at long range. At the time of launch (t minus 0), the automatic launch control system gives the take-off signal after testing about 600 parameters in a few seconds. If all the parameters are within the specified error band, the computer gives a go-ahead signal and the missile takes off. The missile has an onboard computer that carries the specified trajectory which is to be followed by the missile from the time it takes off till it reaches the impact point. Any deviation from the trajectory is detected and quantified by the computer and fed continuously to the control system of the missile. The control system operates the fast reaction thrusters in all the three axes of flight and corrects the deviation and brings the missile to the required trajectory in real-time.

If the corrective action is not done in real-time, the missile will not reach the target and the mission will be a failure. Guidance and control from its onboard computer acts as the brain of the missile. During the flight of the missile, the computer is responsible for guiding the missile to the target to meet the mission requirements and succeed. From this guided missile flight example I would like to share the following experiences:

1. It is necessary for the guidance and control system to monitor the deviation continuously on all the three axes and guide the missile to fly towards the target. The missile control system provides continuous feedback to the missile.

This example reveals that the missile successfully reaches the target *in partnership with* the guidance and control system, which is able to foresee the deviation and provide continuous correction. If the correction is provided after the event is over, you can see that the mission will not succeed.

Similarly, if the auditors audit *after the event is over* or the mission is completed, they will see many deviations which will all be too late to correct. I am sure you can realize the importance of providing online corrections to any deviation.

2. In the development of the missile, 3,000 engineers and staff work in the field of propulsion, aerodynamics, structures, guidance and control, instrumentation and flight simulation. The success of the flight comes from the system design, system integration, configuration management and system management. A dominant group called the quality assurance and quality control group constantly works with the missile team to find the deviations of various sub-systems and systems online—from design to development completion—so that the integrated missile performs to the mission specifications reliably. This is equivalent to a system audit being carried out by the CAG.

Agricultural Mission Model

I would like to illustrate how the CAG can become a partner in a mission right from the commencement of the project. Let us

Public Audit and Good Governance

take the Second Green Revolution as a mission by the Agriculture Ministry as a model.

The Agriculture Ministry has a target of producing around 340 million tonnes of food grain by the year 2020 despite reduced land, reduced availability of water and reduced human resources. Now let us identify the stakeholders. The stakeholders are farmers, agricultural scientists, meteorologists, agricultural planners, seed banks, water and irrigation system managers, organic and inorganic fertilizer manufacturers, chemical and bio-pesticide manufacturers, farm equipment lending agencies, cooperative banking systems and financial institutions, warehouses and godowns, procurement agencies, distribution systems and the coordinating ministries from the central and state governments. The success of the mission is totally dependent on the synchronized integrated action between all the stakeholders and on integrated planning, funding, scheduling and proper execution.

Let me explain the various phases of this mission.

1. For enabling optimum production of food grains from the available land in different regions, the first requirement is the availability of good soil. Once the characteristic of the soil of a particular region is known, the seed (for a particular grain) and fertilizers can be matched to the soil. The first phase of the process would need identification of the land and the type of seed which can be grown on the land, as well as assessing the availability of water.

2. The second phase involves the preparation of the land and the use of fertilizers, leading to seeding and plantation. In this phase, the essential requirements are: availability of right quality seed at the right place, availability of farm equipment, availability of fertilizers, availability of funds through agricultural cooperative banks, proper training to the farmers and transportation system for movement of resources to the desired locations. How do we ensure this? The availability of these resources from the multiple stakeholders of the project is the corrective action for the success of the mission.

3. The third phase involves weeding, the application of pesticides, timely irrigation and the provision of supplementary nutrients for ensuring the healthy growth of the plant. This is totally under the control of the farmer, who works upon advice received from the agricultural scientists. The availability of inputs such as water and pesticides, as well as knowledge inputs are to be ensured in this phase.

4. The fourth phase involves harvesting, movement, storage, timely price fixation, procurement and distribution. In this phase, we have to ensure that the produce is not affected by moisture and rain. Adequate storage facilities need to be available near the villages, in the form of small, medium and big silos. A good transportation system is also required for moving the crops to the market. At this stage, agricultural waste also needs to be converted into products and sold. The

procurement price and processes need streamlining at the right time to ensure that the farmer gets the right revenue for his produce. If there is surplus production, food processing agencies are require to convert the surplus into marketable product by value addition without allowing it to perish.

All these four phases require the fixing of targets, schedules and resource management plans and their proper implementation. In these phases, many of the actions are government driven, such as providing credit to cooperative banks and societies, the provision of adequate quantity of fertilizers for distribution and marketing and the supervision of the quality of seeds, so that adulterated seeds are not deployed. The government, through meteorological research data, has to also announce the period when the monsoon sets in, since it has a direct bearing on the seeding time and timely seeding is essential for ensuring good productivity. This is the open loop system, with stakeholders from different organizations and different motivations.

Successful realization of yearly targets for meeting agricultural goals before 2020 will need coordinated functioning of all the phases of the process. The CAG normally carries out reviews after the task is completed. I would like the CAG to consider *when* it can enter the system, so that they can make effective contributions to the agricultural mission.

Proactive Auditing and Process Control

Now I would like to discuss the future challenges of the CAG.

> Auditing, to the common public, always seems like a mechanism for exposing irregularities. But can auditors be like partners in a partnership firm? I am sure this is possible since both the executives and the auditors are working towards a common cause i.e. the delivery of good governance to citizens. Transparency is the key to good governance. In the world of computers, software developers use process control mechanism, which ensures that the software developed is nearly bug free so that the programmer is prevented from making mistakes. The CAG can perform the same role by developing process controls, guidelines and checks for auditing in the IT environment, so that irregularities will not enter into the financial management of the government and public sector institutions.

Partners in E-governance

The application of ICT (Information Communication Technology) into the audit system should enable the auditors to ensure that the process control mechanism is built into the auditing system. This system would ensure the performance metrics of various domains, such as strategic planning, project management, operational management, risk management practices, business continuity planning, quality of services delivered, customer satisfaction, etc. If the auditors associate themselves with the executives in their e-governance or IT-related programmes, it would also provide credibility and assurance to the stakeholders (in our case, the citizens of the country) about value for money. The CAG team will also be assured of the security within the system, the compliance with standards, the existence of proper process control and integrity in the output.

E-governance Grid for Auditing

The CAG can think of establishing a secure CAG E-governance Grid through broadband network with central and state governments and public sector institutions. In an IT-enabled environment, a near paperless accounting system which hinges on electronic cash and credit card transactions, including authenticated and secure digital signatures, will have to become part and parcel of the business of the CAG. Today, the paper trail is still maintained due to a mistrust of computerization and untested authentication mechanisms. Hence, we merely enter the paper transactions in the computers. This has to be changed in such a way that the transactions are born digitally and automatically captured so that we can spend more time on thinking rather than on data entry. Hence the fusion of ICT and auditing is essential. Since banks and commercial establishments are today already engaged in e-commerce transactions across India, I do not visualize any difficulty in implementing a similar scheme in government departments with qualified encryption standards.

For enabling e-audit through the E-governance Grid the ICT tools needed are:

- Quality Control
- E-auditing System
- Project Management
- Change Management
- Risk Assessment and Control
- Human Resource Planning
- Implementation of near paperless office work flow system
- Performance Tracking System

This will enable the audit team to provide online monitoring of time, cost and the performance and recommend suitable corrective actions for meeting final project goals when the process is in progress. This type of paradigm shift in the approach through auditing will make the CAG a partner in all our time-bound national missions.

Accountants General Can Provide Specific Methodologies

Presently, one of the biggest national challenges is: How do we get maximum economic benefit for the given flow of fund? I believe that this is the core competence of the CAG.

Let me give an instance. The Rural Employment Guarantee Act has been passed by the Parliament. It seeks to provide better job security to the needy in 200 rural districts by giving at least 100 days of guaranteed wage employment in every financial year to every household. How can we make this programme successful based on our earlier experiences? There is a need to link the provision of this Act to the Integrated Rural Development Programme called PURA (Providing Urban Amenities to Rural Areas) as envisaged in the Bharat Nirman programme of the nation.

This is the right time for the CAG to provide e-governance based audit support to central and state governments so that the shortcomings which were noticed in the earlier scheme of rural employment generation are not repeated.

Audit in the World of E-commerce

Our audit system has evolved over many years. But things are changing. The world is fast embracing e-commerce and, very often, one has to deal with faceless entities such as a website. In this world of e-commerce, both the good and the evil coexist. While the advantages of speed and efficiency cannot be questioned, fraud is also equally possible. In India, e-commerce is still at a nascent stage but very soon, it will become a major part of our transactions. It would be necessary for auditors and accountants to generate a policy statement on the 'Best Practices for E-commerce' for the country in partnership with experts. It has become all the more important today since some of our public sector institutions are becoming multinationals, and have assets and businesses in different countries.

Audit in a Borderless World

Many Indian government organizations today set up and acquire companies abroad. The rules and regulations in those countries may be different. What is ethical in another country may be unethical in ours. Auditors and accountants must become specialists in international trade and accounting practices and should be able to seamlessly integrate our practices with the countries with which we trade. Sooner or later, we will see accounting in a borderless world.

Some Suggestions

The members of the CAG have been contributing to the growth and maturity of the system of governance for the last sixty-five years. For enabling members of CAG to become partners in national development, I would like to make the following seven suggestions:

1. The audit teams can work with programme chiefs or executives of national programmes from the very inception of the project. You will find that there may be ten to fifteen critical paths for a ten-year programme. For five-year projects there may be more. The critical paths in the project will be the CAG's audit area.
2. The aim of the audit should be to detect deviations in near real-time while the project is in progress and to provide constructive solutions so that the objective of the project is met well in time.
3. The CAG's experience in the performance audit of welfare schemes should be shared with the relevant ministry, which will enable them to take suitable proactive corrective action while implementing newer schemes.
4. Audit can assist some establishments in disposing off certain inventories of systems of old technologies. Continuous retention of these systems of old technologies involve inefficient use of existing human resource and come in the way of the growth of the organization. Some examples are use of manual drafting systems and conventional lathes and milling machines as opposed to the modern CAD/CAM system that enables direct drafting and feeding of the component into the machine for realizing the product.
5. The CAG may consider the creation and maintenance of a centralized National Asset Register. The salient features of an asset can be put on the website for public awareness.

Periodically, the status of the asset may be reviewed and updated, since the CAG is the custodian of national wealth.

6. The CAG may also consider incorporating a mutually agreed upon online audit system for high value schemes of national importance such as the Rural Employment Scheme, PURA, Golden Quadrilateral, etc. so that maximum value for money is realized in a time-bound manner.
7. Auditors should be sensitive to the fact that e-commerce and a borderless world will soon be a reality and a policy statement will need to be evolved accordingly.

> Auditing, in the modern sense, is a quality assurance phenomenon. It has to move from the conventional quality control mechanism to quality assurance of institutions through the establishment of internal controls and self-controls. An audit has to be proactive and alert the system *before* the occurrence of low performance.

Implementation of the e-governance system in auditing is essential and will assist the CAG to ensure online process control and guidance. This will create close interaction between the auditors and auditees as partners working towards a common goal for providing effective governance to the nation. Apart from the planned audit, the CAG teams must also be observant and be able to detect areas of immediate national concern and find urgent solutions through timely intervention.

Transparency in Defence Missions

Electronic governance enables transparency.

In my decades of experience working in the area of defence research, I have observed the necessity for timely auditing as a way of maintaining efficiency and transparency of defence projects.

The Indian Defence Accounts Service

Given the importance of our defence forces and our defence missions in keeping our nation safe, it is necessary that there is continuous scrutiny and performance audits of these services. The DAD (Defence Accounts Department) has been improving upon the financial management systems of defence services and they have brought in the concept of the performance audit, which has enabled the Defence Ministry to realize higher value from the overall defence outlay.

The study of development programmes and the pointing out of deviations, the investigating of their causes and suggestion of better practices have improved the performance of certain projects. Today, audit is going beyond mere economic aspects and evaluating the efficiency and effectiveness of government programmes.

Both in times of peace and war, the defence audit system has made silent but effective contributions in all fields of the Ministry of Defence. I have had several experiences where valuable and timely advice from financial experts enabled our project teams of scientists, technologists and managers to maintain the momentum of defence projects.

Defence Accounts As Partners of Defence Missions

Financial advice and audit teams can work with programme chiefs or executives of defence programmes right from the inception of the project and participate in the study of the feasibility of the project. In this respect, I would like to discuss how the defence accounts effectively participated in an important programme that went through difficult times.

This incident took place in 1998. In 1992, the Light Combat Aircraft team decided to go for digital Fly-by-Wire Control System (FCS) for the aircraft. This was needed to increase the required maneuverability of the aircraft. At that time, the country did not have experience in developing FCS. The only two countries who had the necessary experience were France and the US. The French company (Dassault System) had expertise in hybrid systems whereas our need was for an all digital Fly-by-Wire. Hence, it was thought appropriate to have a US partner who had the capability for design, development and integration of FCS on fighter aircraft. There were three candidates: General Electric Company that later became LMCS (Lockheed Martin Control Systems, now called BAe Systems), Lear Astronics and Bendix. Finally, we chose LMCS for the contract since they had experience in designing FCS for the F-16 aircraft. A joint team for design and development of the FCS was formed with ADE (Aeronautical Development Establishment) and LMCS. The work share of the Indian team and the LMCS team were identified. The evolution of the system requirements was a joint effort. The prototype flight control computer was to be done by ADE, while flight certification was to be provided by LMCS.

The contract progressed slowly between 1992 and 1998. The department of defence finance was constantly monitoring and providing an impetus to the progress of the contract. Then, as you all are aware, India carried out its nuclear test on 11 May 1998. As soon as this event occurred, the American government imposed technological sanctions. Due to the sanctions, LMCS broke the contract and retained all the Indian equipment, software and the technical information which were in their premises.

This was definitely a shock for the Indian team. Immediately, I called for a meeting of the directors of Aeronautical Development Agency (ADA), National Aerospace Laboratories (NAL), Aeronautical Development Establishment, Centre for Artificial Intelligence and Robotics (CAIR), Hindustan Aeronautics Limited (HAL), National Flight Test Centre as well as Professor I.G. Sharma, a renowned control system specialist, Professor T.K. Ghoshal, a noted digital control system expert, and guidance and control specialists from DRDO and ISRO, along with our financial advisors. The FCS team explained to these members the situation that now arose due to the unilateral termination of contract by LMCS. The finance team participated in all the discussions. We had a full day of discussion on the methodology which was now needed to be followed in order to successfully complete the development of the FCS. The team, after prolonged deliberation, gave a structured method by which the development could be completed and the system could be certified for flight trials. They also mentioned that they would support the programme and work in whatever capacity they had to with the ADE and ADA teams. The financial advisors of DRDO and ADA also came forward to provide financial support to the development tasks. They also proceeded to undertake appropriate action against LMCS for the unilateral termination of the contract.

Based on the recommendations of the specialists, we immediately strengthened the ADE software team with ten additional experienced software engineers from the ADA. ADA was given the responsibility of the verification and validation of the software. An integrated flight control system review committee was constituted with the director of ADE as the chairman and the program director of ADA as the co-chair to support development and resolve all conflicts arising between the Control Law Team, Software, Hardware and Simulation. This team met once a week and brought out all the issues arising in different work centres and solutions were found. In addition, a review team was formed with project director (Flight Control System) as chairman with members from HAL, ADA, ADE, CEMILAC and test pilots from the National Flight Test Centre as members. This team also met every week and resolved all the problems arising in the development and tests of the system. We also introduced the participation of the certification agency (CEMILAC) and the inspection agency (CRI) in all these reviews. The aim was to make sure that any problem in any of the systems was brought into focus at the earliest so that a solution could be found.

In addition, we made it a point to have a special agenda in the monthly technical committee meeting on the development of the integrated flight control system wherein the directors of ADE, NAL, National Flight Test Centre and the general manager of HAL presented the progress of the project and its problems. Confidence building took place by intensifying the tests. For example, informal tests were carried out over 1,000 hours and the formal test was conducted over 150 hours. Similarly, the pilot flew the simulator for more than 2,000 hours. Thus, what we missed from the foreign partner, we compensated by enhancing the critical design review and increasing the test time to ensure a safe man-rated design of the integrated flight control system.

The entire team took the cancellation of the contract as a national challenge. If earlier it was going to take three years, we were going to do it in two years. If it was to take twenty million dollars, we would do it in ten. We would work twenty-four hours a day to complete the task.

> That was the time I realized the power of the Indian scientific community and the need for the partnership of defence finance department in the progress of our country. I realized that no country could dominate us by imposing technological sanctions or economic sanctions. The collective power of our scientific, managerial and financial management team would defeat challenges from any nation.
>
> Today, I can proudly say that our scientists have designed, developed, tested, evaluated and integrated the flight control system in the LCA, which has logged more than 2,528 trouble-free flight sorties in fourteen different aircraft with 1,620 flying hours.

The challenge of the development was that the aircraft of this class was being designed for the first time and we introduced the state-of-the-art digital Fly-by-Wire technology in the very first prototype, which is often unstable. We developed the final hardware and software required for testing and evaluation of the control system in the aircraft on our own after the foreign partner left the scene and our own certification team, which had no experience in certifying Fly-by-Wire aircraft, gained confidence and certified the aircraft as flight worthy. Above all, the pilots, who had never flown a prototype, flew the aircraft based on their flying experience in the simulator.

Honest self-assessment, identification of the area of uncertainty and dedicated efforts to solve problems were an important aspect of this programme. Integrating the strength of our industry and academia, along with R&D labs, the Air Force and the Defence Accounts Department, we could achieve what was perceived to be an impossible task.

This is a demonstration of the Indian will, of the 'can-do' spirit.

With respect to the LCA, I would like to mention another important feature. The full scale of the engineering development Phase I of the programme was sanctioned at a cost of ₹2,188 crore. While sanctioning the programme in 1993, we envisaged building two prototypes only, namely TD-1 and TD-2. Later, the ADA team, in partnership with the defence finance department, revised the programme by increasing the number of prototypes from two to four. This was acclaimed as one of the important milestones for the LCA and the people who participated in this great work were K.P. Rao, R. Ramanathan and Siva Subramaniam. This could be achieved because of the online collective decision-making system instituted by them for the programme. During the commencement of the programme, it was proposed that many items be imported. While the programme advanced, the project team, in consultation with the finance department, resorted to indigenous development and manufacture of those items, leading to a substantial savings in cost. Also, the development of the Carbon Fibre Composites wing was contracted for half the planned amount through hard negotiations.

In all these areas, there was an excellent partnership between scientists, technologists, user service and the finance department. In the LCA management system, the secretary (Defence Finance) was a member of both the general body and the governing council. The Additional Finance Advisor from DRDO was a member of the technical committee. This close-knit system enabled the indigenous programme to become a success.

Another important financial decision-making which happened in the year 1989 was a system of concurrent R&D and current production approvals. In defence research projects, usually R&D finance approval is done first, followed by that for production. By doing this simultaneously not only was time saved but it also showed faith in the R&D team by assuming that their work would be good enough to go in for production. At that time we had just conducted only one successful flight test of Prithvi. When the project team met A.K. Ghosh, then the financial advisor (Defence Service), in spite of financial constraints for various activities in the defence budget, he found the funds for concurrent production of the Prithvi system at the right time. This was a major breakthrough in the missile programme. Today, two strategic missiles are in production because of the right type of design and the collaboration with the defence finance department.

Defence Accounts and the India 2020 Vision

Richa Misra, Jt. IFA, had asked me at a lecture, 'What role does Defence Accounts play in achieving the India 2020 vision?'

My reply was that the Defence Ministry is one with a large expenditure budget. We have seen that the Defence R&D, Defence Production, Defence Training Centres and Maintenance Centres have huge capacities. Every year, the Department of Defence Production, through its defence production centres and ordnance factories, produce billions of dollars worth of product and systems for the country. The time has now come for removing the so-called veil of secrecy and the need for aggressive marketing of certain products, systems, training and maintenance packages in the international market. Defence products have to be marketed through public-private partnership enterprises. The DAD has to evolve a methodology for marketing defence products in the international market. Since the defence budget is more than 20 per cent of the national budget, the Defence Ministry has the responsibility of aggressively marketing defence systems in the international market and reducing the financial burden. This, in turn, will assist our vision of India 2020.

E-governance and Defence Accounts

I have noticed a press report that mentions the ten best government intranets in the world. I found that the Defence, Finance and Accounting services of the US finds first place in this report. I am sure that with the core competence available in our country in the IT, finance and accounts sectors, Indian defence finance can definitely aspire to become the best intranet in the country and even the world. We can think of establishing a secure CGDA (Controller General of Defence Accounts) E-governance Grid through VPN broadband network with the Army, Navy, Air Force, Defence R&D and the Department of Defence Production. In an IT-enabled environment, a near paperless e-governance and accounting system which hinges on electronic transactions, including authenticated and secure digital signatures, will have to become part and parcel of the business of the CGDA. In this connection, I would like to suggest that the CGDA consider the issuing of credit cards to units for managing their cash assignments and imprest account.

Some Suggestions

Finance advisors have to transform themselves into system finance managers. That means, instead of looking at a part of the system, they should have the entire system in focus. The performance and cost PERTs (Programme Evaluation and Review Technique) of the project or programme have to be the common reference point for the finance and audit, R&D, production and service communities. While I was secretary to the Department of Defence R&D (1992-2000), R. Ramanathan was my financial advisor. He would clear any file with his views within a day or maximum three days. Speedy and thoughtful action are vital in mission-mode operations. The finance team needs to advise on how to do it rather than how not to do it.

The members of the Defence Accounts Service have been contributing to the growth and the maturity of the governance system of the Defence Ministry for the last 250 years. For enabling members of the CGDA to become partners in national security, I would like to make the following five suggestions:

1. Is it right to allow audit queries to graduate into audit paras and audit paras transform into oral evidence before PAC? I am sure with an intensive partnership between the user, the Defence R&D, Defence Production and Supplies, Defence Finance and CAG, we can think of an online real-time deviation detection mechanism for the resolution of procedural errors cropping up in the system. Here, I would like to give an example. When I took over DRDO in 1982, there were over 1,500 pending audit queries, and more than twenty audit paras with many of them having the potential to become oral evidence cases by PAC. Members including scientists, Defence Accounts members and CAG and myself worked for three days, studied all the files and

asked for clarifications. It was found that in some cases the technical teams had not explained the problem to the audit team properly and in some cases, the audit team did not have the full understanding of the technical necessity. After clarifications and discussions, the task team reduced the number of audit queries to less than ten and audit paras went into revision. This shows how an intensive partnership between finance, audit and users can create a robust error-free management system in establishments.

2. The Defence Accounts Department is a service organization. The service provider has the responsibility to provide full satisfaction to clients or customers. The total CGDA system must be designed to provide customer satisfaction with a high degree of effectiveness and efficiency and with minimum wastage. This I found was happening in all the defence establishments I have visited, even in Siachen. The pay requirements of jawans are not delayed. Also, pension benefits are paid on the day the person goes into retirement.

3. Defence Accounts can assist service establishments and production agencies in disposing of certain inventories of systems of old technologies.

4. With ICT playing an important role in every sphere of organizational activity, the CGDA may also consider introduction of electronic filing of claims by service personnel and establishments. To start with, TA/DA claims, LTC, provident fund advance claims could be introduced.

5. There are a number of financial advice, accounting and auditing organizations in the country, both in the private and public domain. It might be useful to create a common platform among all these organizations to know of innovations made in different organizations. The CGDA could take the initiative in creating such a forum where specialists from different organizations could work together and evolve areas which could then be emulated by sister organizations. This interaction and interchange of ideas would enable enrichment of all organizations through the cross-fertilization of ideas.

Governance for Every Citizen

Where there is righteousness in the heart,
there is beauty in the character.

Changing Nation

I have seen three Indias in my lifetime. The first was in my childhood, when India was under a foreign colonial rule struggling to gain independence. It was a vision for independence led by great leaders like Mahatma Gandhi, Pandit Nehru and many other leaders.

The second was India post-1947, which was independent but still strived for recognition internationally and recovering from the losses of colonial rule. It was an India that hoped that one day, the nation will establish self sufficiency in food, have a strong economy, and the respect in the international arena that it truly deserves. Many leaders, scientists, servicemen and social reformers chiselled the nation for decades bringing it to its present glory—economic development with social equity and a vibrant democracy.

Then I saw the third India, an era which belongs to the youth. It is a land of opportunities, of growth at previously unimaginable rates, of a strong work force, of technological leadership. Six decades ago, few would have ventured to imagine that this nation of diversity, often termed as an experiment in democracy, would eventually find its place amongst the top economies of the world, would have world-class educational institutions and would be the first to discover water on the lunar surface.

The three Indias I have witnessed are very different from one another and of course, there are still many issues which we as citizens have to address, including poverty, illiteracy and corruption.

To achieve the goals of providing good governance to all and making India a fully developed nation, a national movement for development is essential. In this movement, every citizen, every constituent of our democracy has to participate. What can be the profile for people's participation in this movement? Citizen's participation can be in many important areas like:

- Reaching the unreached
- Human resource development
- Entrepreneurship development
- Role of women
- Environment
- Participation of the youth in the political system

Reaching the Unreached: Rural Development

The government has increased credit availability in the agriculture sector. NABARD and banking and financial institutions have to work together to find hassle-free methods of providing micro credit and micro investment to needy farmers, so that they are weaned away from the clutches of elements which exploit them. Simultaneously, agricultural researchers, extension workers from academic institutions, non-governmental organizations and industry should work closely with farmers and enable them to increase productivity, storage, food processing and marketing. In addition, they should facilitate farmers to undertake non-farm tasks on the lines of 'one product per village cluster' scheme in order to promote the export of products based on the core competence of the village, which will increase the sustainability of the rural sector as a whole. Insurance companies have to come forward with micro insurance, crop insurance and cattle insurance, apart from low-cost medical insurance, for providing risk cover to farmers.

Similarly, units like mobile diagnostic clinics such as those in Uttarakhand may be operated in all districts to enable medical care to reach the unreached.

Recently, I have come across a number of initiatives by our judicial systems at various levels for the speedy delivery of justice through legal aid clinics, mediation and conciliation, mobile courts and lok-adalats and by increasing the number of working days and number of hours of working per day. These initiatives can be reinforced by having mobile courts reaching the village to deliver justice at the doorstep of rural citizens.

The corporate sector may also think of reaching out to rural sectors for development as an essential component of Corporate Social Responsibility. In a world dominated by communication, extending communication from the privileged to the unreached should be part of our processes of technological upheaval.

Human Resource Development

Presently our university education system contributes 3 million graduates and post graduates every year and students seeking employment after completion of 10th and 10+2 are around 7 million per year. Thus, nearly 10 million youth come into the employment market every year. In the 21st century, India needs a large number of talented youth with higher education for the tasks of knowledge acquisition, knowledge imparting, knowledge creation and knowledge sharing. At present, India has millions of youth under the age of twenty-five. This will grow continuously till the year 2050. Keeping this in mind, the universities and educational systems should create two cadres of personnel: (i) a global cadre of skilled youth with specific knowledge of special skills (ii) a global cadre of youth with higher education. These two cadres will be required not only for powering the manufacturing and service sectors of India but also fulfilling the human resource requirements of various countries. Thus, universities and the secondary school education system will have to work towards increasing the number of students passing through their systems.

Other Indians who are not covered by the higher education system should also have world-class skill sets in areas such as construction, carpentry, electrical systems, repair of mechanical systems, fashion design, para-legal, para-medical, accountancy, sales and marketing, software and hardware maintenance and service and software quality assurance—to name a few. Every Indian should have either a world-class higher education or world-class skill sets.

This is an important task in which all universities, academic specialists, colleges, vocational training institutions, certification agencies, banking systems and industrial enterprises can contribute in terms of assessing correct numbers, designing courses related to nation-building, assessing and providing infrastructural requirement, improving the quality of teachers, ensuring teacher-student ratio, complementing classroom education with virtual knowledge through tele-education and, above all, ensuring that students are able to face international competition in employable skills.

Systems must be designed in such a way that no aspiring competent student should be denied a quality education. The system of education must also maintain a certain uniform standard.

These are examples of what the government has to do to

provide an enabling environment where our youth can use their knowledge skills in making the nation prosperous.

Entrepreneurship Development

Orientation for entrepreneurship has to start right from the schools. Teachers need to highlight the role of entrepreneurship for national development for schools. During college, students must be exposed to business development opportunities and must be trained towards the creation of new enterprises. Parents should encourage their children to take up new ventures after their education. We should cultivate a mindset that 'Idea is wealth'.

The government must create a facilitating environment for the provision of venture capital for innovative ideas without collateral security. Universities and engineering and management institutions should work with banks and other funding agencies towards simplifying procedures for setting up businesses and working with entrepreneurs till the project becomes self-sustaining and viable. Procedures in government should facilitate the spotting and recognition of new Indian talent in entrepreneurship by creating a level playing field for healthy competition. Citizens who can afford it, should turn themselves into angel investors or start venture capital organizations to fund such new ventures. Big and small industries need to have an open mind in order to encourage and partner with young entrepreneurs.

Role of Women

Women have an important role to play in shaping both the family and the nation. They have much to contribute for societal upliftment. I have come across a project called Siruthuli which has been taken up in Coimbatore. This project on large-scale rainwater harvesting and rejuvenating the water bodies, afforestation, sewage and waste water treatment and solid waste management integrates a large number of people from different walks of life. A home-maker is providing the leadership to this project. Similarly, SEWA is another organization started by a woman that has helped improve the lives of a large number of women in Gujarat. There are many more examples like this across the country.

Many of the panchayats across the country have women members who have been giving leadership in various rural development initiatives. Imagine the difference which can be made in our 600,000 villages with such actions.

Environment

The environment can be cleaned up only through countrywide active participation of citizens. People as a team can participate in cleaning up the environment. The cleaning of the Kali Bein river in Punjab is one such example. Spiritual leaders can play a very important role in persuading devotees about the importance of the clean environment movement, which in turn, will promote the evolution of beautiful minds. Local groups can be formed to spread awareness about cleanliness in residential areas. Welfare associations, NCC cadets, scouts, guides and NSS volunteers can proactively form these groups.

Industrialists should follow the prescribed norms for environmental standards in all their institutions and make buildings friendly to differently abled people. Government employees should keep their offices and their environment clean. Parents and teachers should emphasize the need for environmentally friendly measures to younger citizens. Citizens can plant trees and nurture them in their neighbourhood every year.

Our public infrastructure, airports, railway stations, bus stations, sea ports and hospitals form the face of the nation in the global environment. It is the responsibility of all stakeholders, including the citizens, to promote cleanliness in all these public facilities.

Participation of the Youth in the Political System

The youth should take up politics as their career in large numbers. Political Science should form part of the curriculum from secondary to college level for all students, with developmental politics as the focus. Citizens should proactively cast their votes to select candidates who are known to perform with honesty. Legal experts and professionals should educate citizens about the political process, the Constitution, and their rights and responsibilities.

Similarly, there are many more important tasks like making education accessible to every citizen, uplifting citizens below the poverty line through a focused mission and accelerating agriculture reforms. In the same way, there can be a movement in the judiciary for time-bound clearance of pending cases. The judiciary and bar should ensure that the common citizen gets speedy justice with nobility.

While citizens demand that our police force has to be transparent and action-oriented, it is also essential that police stations are electronically connected and simultaneously the police force are empowered with better quality of life like proper housing, sanitary facilities, medical cover and children's education. This will enable them to concentrate on their work with peace of mind and thereby the output from the police force would increase.

Above all, women constitute fifty per cent of our population. Their dignity should be protected and they should get proper representation in all decision-making institutions. Our panchayats truly represent the village citizens and they should ensure that all funds allotted for rural development in their area are properly utilized for the intended purpose.

National Security

Our armed forces and paramilitary forces are awake day or night guarding our borders on land, in air and at sea. They remain vigilant to counter any threat and facilitate unhindered progress of national development. I have experienced this personally when I visited the Siachen Glacier that is at an altitude of 17,000 ft. The temperature of minus 35 degrees Centigrade with heavy winds did not deter our courageous jawans.

Another time, when I was in an Indian Navy submarine, I saw young sailors and naval officers functioning efficiently and vigilantly in the silent underwater environment, keeping all-round vigil on their mission in the Indian Ocean.

When I was with the 20 Squadron of the Indian Air Force, I saw first hand how our fighter pilots could meet any challenge of multi-targets through radar missiles and EW systems. We cherish the valour, commitment and devotion to duty of these gallant personnel of our armed forces.

Our police forces, paramilitary and intelligence agencies complement each other to provide safety and security to our citizens from criminals and extremists. Many members of these forces have laid down their lives while protecting the people, the flag and nation. We salute them all.

Our colleges and universities must not only generate excellent entrepreneurs and researchers but also the best soldiers for our country. Parents should encourage their children to participate in national security missions.

> An economically developed India by 2020 is a mission for over a billion people, where every one of us has a role to play. It will only be a reality if everyone, particularly the youth, asks oneself, 'What can I give?' My interactions with our citizens in India and abroad, particularly the youth, has demonstrated to me the positive energy flowing in individuals that makes them eager to give all they can to make India economically developed. The attitude of giving by every citizen and each group will definitely be an enriching factor for the whole nation, leading to an accelerated development process. When the nation marches towards its missions, many challenges will come on the way. Courage, in all sections of society, is a very important trait in overcoming these challenges.

I would like to narrate an incident. On 8 June 2006, I was in the Su-30-MKI aircraft. The captain of the aircraft was Wing Commander Ajay Rathore. The duration of the flight was forty minutes. I participated in all the flight actions. When I landed, there were many youth and media personnel present. One young man asked me a question, 'Sir, you flew in the supersonic fighter aircraft at the age of seventy-four. Were you afraid at any time during the flight?' I told the young man, 'In all the forty minutes of the flight, I was busy on the controls and instruments and experiencing the g build up. I was advised by the captain to track targets and also look at the ground using the synthetic aperture radar. In addition, I was observing the performance of the instruments developed indigenously. I was continuously busy in flight operations and I didn't have time to allow fear to enter into me.'

Dear friends, how many of you have the 'I can do it' spirit?

This is the song of youth that millions of young Indians have repeated after me:

As a young citizen of India,
Armed with technology, knowledge and love for my nation,
I realize small aim is a crime.

I will work and sweat for a great vision—
The vision of transforming India into a developed nation,
Powered by economic strength with value system.

I am one of the citizens of the billion;
Only vision will ignite a billion souls.
It has entered into me.
The ignited soul, compared to any resource, is the
Most powerful resource on the earth,
Above the earth and under the earth.

The Vision for a New India

Many civilizations collapsed and many nations failed because they did not have the vision at the right time.

In the last many years, I have met 17 million youth in all parts of the country. Some incidents from these interactions stand out in my mind.

Dynamics of the Mind of the Youth

On 19 Jan 2011, I visited Amravati to attend a programme organized by the Satpuda Shikshan Prasarak Mandal to address one lakh youth. I gave a talk, 'I am Unique', in the presence of many political and societal development leaders, teachers and educationists. After I finished my lecture, among many other questions, an interesting question came from a rural boy.

He introduced himself as a tenth standard student from Harali village. He asked, 'Sir, our media and my friends always say that China's economy is progressing better and faster than

India. Tell me, sir, why can't India's develop faster? Also tell us what we, the youth, should do?'

There was great applause for this boy's question, which meant that the crowd of one lakh young people needed a right answer from me. My friends on the dais, too, were looking to me for an answer. Reflecting for a brief moment, I asked the boy what his name was. He said his name was Vineet. I said, 'Vineet, you have a powerful mind and you also love your nation. My answer to you is: it is true that the economic progress made by China and India are reportedly quite different. But India is following a system of parliamentary democracy, elected by the people. Democracy has its ups and downs, but we must keep flying. The associated delays have to be removed through good leadership. But I want to ask all the youth assembled here, suppose I give two systems: one with full democracy and with a high pace of development, and the other, a political system like China's, which one would you like to choose?'

When I asked them to lift their hands, 99 per cent of the youth lifted their hands and said that they wanted a democracy with a faster rate of growth.

> The message here is that the youth want democracy to be re-invented with faster growth. The young mind is turbulent and looking for a vision for the nation and its fast accomplishment. It is very important to engage young minds with an inspiring vision for thinking and action.

'When Can I Sing a Song of India?'

During the last few years, I have seen how the India Vision 2020 has inspired people, particularly the youth of the nation.

I recall a situation in 1990 where I was interacting with the youth of Ahmedabad. One girl there asked me a question, 'When can I sing a song of India?' At that time, her brother, who was in the United States, was always talking about how the United States was best at everything. This girl sitting in India was fed up with her brother's stories and in her quest to find an answer asked, 'When can I sing a song of India?'

How did I answer? I explained to her the India Vision 2020 and told her, 'Have confidence and certainly you can sing a song of India by 2020.'

But for the last few years, while interacting with the youth, I have been seeing a marked change in the thinking. From a notion of what can the nation offer me, they have been asking me, 'What can I give to the nation?' That means the youth are ready to contribute towards national development. Recently, I have observed a further change. There is more confidence among our young people. For instance, during my address in Shillong in 2013, a youth told me, 'I can do it, we can do it and the nation can do it.' With the youth actively participating in the developmental process, I am sure that India will be transformed into a developed nation before the year 2020.

I would like to focus on three aspects of this participation for the youth in governance: the birth of a vision, the current ambience in India and its challenges and finally, the mission to graduate the nation into an economically developed nation.

The Birth of a Vision

Let me share with you my unique experience of the formulation of the Vision 2020 strategies in the mid 1990s. I was given the task of chairing the TIFAC (Technology Information Forecasting and Assessment Council). I recollect that in the first meeting of the council, we took a decision that the TIFAC must evolve a plan as to how India can be transformed into an economically developed nation by the year 2020. When the suggestion was mooted, everybody wondered how we could evolve such a long-term mission under the prevailing economic and social conditions of the country. That was the time when Prime Minister Narasimha Rao had just announced the economic liberalization and growth measures for the Indian economy and its impact was starting to be felt.

In spite of this, the council, with many young members, jumped to the idea and we discussed for one full day how we could translate thought into action. At a time when the economy was growing at around 5 to 6 per cent per annum in GDP, we had to envisage a growth rate of at least 10 per cent per annum consistently for over ten years for realizing the development vision of 2020. This challenge ignited the minds of all of us in the council. The members of the TIFAC council at that time included the principal secretary to the prime minister, the nine secretaries to the government of India, the chiefs of CII, ASSOCHAM and FICCI, the chairman of IDBI, ICICI, IFCI, the chairman of Public Sector Corporations, the chief executives of a number of private sector institutions, the vice chancellors of different universities and scientists from the Department of Science and Technology. We debated and arrived at seventeen task teams with over 500 members, who consulted with over 5,000 people in various sectors of the economy.

Committees worked for over two years, resulting in twenty-five reports which we presented to the then prime minister on 2 Aug 1996. The reports included vision on areas such as agro-food processing, advance sensors, civil aviation, electric power, waterways, road transportation, tele-communications, food and agriculture, engineering industries, healthcare, life science and biotechnology, materials and processing, electronics and communications, chemical process industry, services, strategic industry and driving forces. Transforming India into a developed nation implied that every citizen of the country would live well above the poverty line, their education and health would be of a high standard, national security would be assured and core competence in certain major areas would enable production of quality goods competitively for export and for bringing all-round prosperity for countrymen.

Impediments to the National Vision

As I see it, some of the impediments to Vision 2020 are as follows:

The vision document was prepared at the time of Prime Minister Narasimha Rao. The document was given to Prime Minister Atal Bihari Vajpayee. Vajpayeeji announced in the Parliament and also announced at the Independence Day address at the Red Fort that India will become an economically developed nation before 2020. In the governors' conference during my presidency, Prime Minister Manmohan Singh also announced that his government will work for an economically developed nation and he assured all the governors of the states.

My experience says that Vision 2020 does not belong to a party, a government or an individual. It is the national vision. It has to be discussed in detail by all elected representatives of the nation for a few weeks in the Parliament and they should debate, discuss and assent so that a national consensus will emerge within all the stakeholders of the vision—including the executive, the judiciary, political leaders, the media, the academia, the business industry, the medical community, farmers, the youth and the people of the nation. For this reason, there should be a commitment towards the national vision from every individual in all walks of life.

If it takes fifteen years for the realization of such a vision document, it means that three democratically elected governments have to work together to realize this vision, although the methodology may be different. National missions cannot be a part of a party agenda, but it *can* be a part of its election manifesto and should be realized. The vision needs to be approved by the Parliament, so that there will remain a continuity in its progress, irrespective of the period of the three governments.

Hence the elected leader of the nation should be a creative leader, who walks the path of pursuing developmental politics, adopting cooperation and collaboration as the key to operational procedure and using the core competence of all parties—irrespective of party affiliations—as well as other able minds and creative minds from any discipline to realize the vision of an economically developed nation.

Current Ambience in India

Now, let me provide a visualization of India as an economically developed India by the year 2020. The Indian economy was growing at an average of 9 per cent per annum till the year 2008. In 2009-10, the Indian economy was affected due to global economic turbulence, but nevertheless it grew at over 7 per cent in the year of global recession. Even when the economic zones of the US and the Europe still looked bleak, India grew at about 6.9 per cent in the last quarter of 2011. In 2013, the GDP growth was at the 5.5 per cent mark.

I was asking myself what type of innovation is needed to enrich the Indian economy and other world economies under the present circumstances. I had discussions on this subject with several economic experts. It came to light that the Indian economy can withstand the world financial crisis better. This is due to:

- The liberalization process in India has checks and balances consistent with the unique social requirements of the country.
- The Indian banking system has always been conservative, which has prevented a crisis similar to that in the USA and in Europe.
- The Indian psyche is generally savings oriented and living within one's means is a part of the Indian mindset.
- The 400-million middle class, with its purchasing power, is providing economic stability to the nation.

Therefore, India is able to withstand the global economic crisis to a certain extent, but we are still vulnerable to the vagaries of the global economic turbulence because of an excess of imports and reduced exports, leading to trade deficit, increased current account deficit—which leads to inflation—and the depreciation of the rupee to 60.49 per US dollar in June 2013. If the US banks fail, the Indian economy is affected. If EU faces economic crisis, we see its effect on the Indian economy.

Why does this happen even though India has a good economic foundation? It is because we have an economic system which is vulnerable to the fluctuations of the world economy and our economic growth is not sustainable, as witnessed from the 5 per cent GDP growth in the 1990s to 9 per cent for around four years till 2009 and finally the present 5.5 per cent. This is mainly due to our prevailing economic policies which are stifling the growth of agriculture and food processing, the manufacturing sector and the service sector. If we bring a marked change in our socio-political and economic policies with a focus on inclusiveness, then I am confident that we as a nation will be able to overcome the economic crisis and progress to new heights.

What Has India Achieved?

We have only six years left in order to achieve the goals of Vision 2020. The nation should take this as its primary task, and facilitate all stakeholders to contribute towards realizing the goals of this mission.

The India Vision 2020 is progressing; today India has made substantial progress in enhancing agricultural productivity and increasing per capita income. According to NASSCOM, the IT–BPO sector in India aggregated revenues of USD 100 billion in FY2012, where export and domestic revenue stood at USD 69.1 billion and USD 31.7 billion respectively, growing by over

The Vision for a New India

9 per cent. The pharma industry has grown to USD 20 billion. The ISRO-enabled mission to find water on the moon through Chandrayaan-1 was undertaken and the Mars Orbiter Mission is on its way to the orbit of the Red Planet. India is the world's second-largest mobile phone user with 900 million users. The Indian automobile industry has become the third largest in the world with 2.8 million automobile vehicles produced in 2013.

Large-scale infrastructure has also been created as a part of rural and urban development missions such as the multi-lane Golden Quadrilateral roadways and the development of airport infrastructure in all metro cities. All rural roads are getting developed at the state level as well.

The current literacy rate in India stands at 74.04 per cent. India's healthcare sector is projected to grow to nearly USD 40 billion and quality healthcare infrastructure is projected to reach all states by 2015. We are also aspiring to provide clean green energy and safe drinking water to all the citizens of the nation.

With this growth, we have to assess where we are in terms of what we aspired to in the 1990s, and where the gap is. It is time for the nation and its leaders to take up a review mission to assess the gap and suggest methods by which we can accelerate progress so that by 2020, India can become a developed country with:

- Zero poverty
- 100 per cent literacy
- Quality healthcare for all

- Value system embedded quality education for all
- Value added employment for every citizen consistent with education and professional skills.

If we channelize our integrated efforts towards the development of India before 2020, then the growth of the nation is certain.

Economically Developed Nation and its Missions

Based on my interaction with various intellectuals, experts and researchers from universities in India and abroad and students and faculty from IIMs Ahmedabad, Indore, Bangalore and Shillong and with the millions of students of the nation, let me propose the following action points for realizing our goal of an economically developed nation:

Sustainable Rural Development

PURA: Based on both private institutional and government efforts, PURA has become a proven model for sustainable rural development. Hence for bringing all around sustainable development, India needs to launch the Integrated National PURA Mission to create 7,000 PURA clusters across the nation, which will empower Indians and bring sustainable development in rural and urban areas. Every year we spend more than ₹100,000 crores for national development. Part of those funds can be directed towards realizing the 7,000 PURA clusters.

Energy Independence, Clean and Green Environment and Water Management

Energy: It is essential for the Indian Parliament to announce the Energy Independence Mission by 2030. Power generation through renewable energy has to be increased from 5 per cent to 28 per cent. Dependence on fossil fuels as primary energy source needs to be brought under 50 per cent from the present 75 per cent. Mandating the use of ethanol from 10 per cent to 20 per cent and the associated public policy for ethanol development by the sugarcane industry is also required. There is also a need for a sustainable biofuel policy for generating 60 million tonnes of biofuel, along with the use of alternate sources such as emulsification, bio algae and hydrogen fuel.

Environment: Enacting an inclusive environment enrichment policy instead of the prevailing extractive environment protection policy is required. We also need to increase the forest cover from 20 per cent to 40 per cent by 2020 as well as enrich the environment through mandatory zero liquid discharge and zero effluent discharge system policy for industrial waste, encourage power generation from biomass and municipal waste at city corporations and village municipalities and create 200,000 carbon neutral village panchayats before 2020.

Waterways: We need the implementation of the Smart Waterways Grid across India to harness 1500 BCM of floodwater and connect the rivers and catchment areas as a single plane. The Grid will receive 1500 BCM of floodwater and act as a water Grid so that water can be released to any deficient place and replenished during flood. It would act as a 15,000 km national reservoir. It would be able to provide drinking water to 600 million people, irrigation to 150 million acres of land, and generate 60,000 MW of power. Due to ground water recharge, it would also save 4000 MW of power. Each state can implement this mission with an outlay of approximately ₹50,000 crores with annual budgetary support, central government assistance, public private consortium and with support from the World Bank in a BOOT (Build, Operate, Own and Transfer) based PPP model and this can be realized within 2020.

Apart from this, an Integrated Water Resource Management system is also required to revive water bodies and tanks and build farm ponds and check dams across India as well as increase irrigation infrastructure and ground water potential, thereby enhancing the safe drinking water resources of the nation.

Agriculture, Manufacturing and Service Sector

Agriculture: In this sector, we need to launch the Second Green Revolution mission as an integrated agriculture, industry and service sector programme with an aim of 10 per cent growth rate in agriculture before 2020 and produce a minimum of 340 million tonnes of food as opposed to the present 250 million tonnes despite reduced water, land and human power environment. Technologies such as SSI (Sustainable Sugarcane Initiative) and SRI (System of Rice Intensification), precision farming, a system-oriented approach and technologically advanced pre and post harvesting equipment usage will more than double agricultural productivity and ensure the 30 per cent contribution to GDP by 2020 from the present 15 per cent.

The introduction of the innovative Community Cooperative Farming Model for identifying crops in selected regions based on the characterization of the soil condition and ensuring that quality input material is available at the right time will also be beneficial. The industry sector has to be empowered with inclusive growth-oriented policies to set up farm level silos, cold chain, refrigerated transportation, food processing industries, etc.

Manufacturing: The manufacturing industry has to be empowered in order to achieve a 25 per cent GDP contribution by 2020 from the 16 per cent as of 2012. A proactive National Manufacturing Policy is the need of the hour.

It is essential to restructure viable industries with technology, business process and human resource. Proactive public policy is essential to relieve financial stress, provide liquidity support and save the productive assets of the country.

We need Global Skill Development for the youth to take up value-added employment in manufacturing and service sectors. An inclusive policy for the adoption of state-of-the-art technology, machines and standards by the industry is essential. Ensuring the availability of energy, capital and logistic transportation for reducing production cost and thereby making the product competitive in the global market will lead to a reduction of inflation. Establishing innovation ecosystems is essential for the growth of the manufacturing and service industries.

Education and Healthcare

School Education: Quality input generates quality output. The primary foundation for such action is the quality of teachers at the school level—from the primary to the higher secondary level. The creation of a revamped National Quality Teacher Education System and its associated inclusive policy is essential. What we need is a creative syllabus, creative teachers and creative classrooms for value-based quality school education.

Higher Education: The higher education system has to focus on research and development at the university level. Instead of monitoring and control by agencies such as UGC and AICTE, we should allow higher educational institutions to compete internationally by setting their educational standards at par with world-class institutions so that they can be rated by independent agencies with a pool of eligible experts in the field on rotation. A minimum criteria may be set up for achieving excellence.

The Vision for a New India

Research and Development in Higher Education: Removing red tapism and favoritism in higher education and research administration and management is of utmost importance. We need to empower universities, both government funded and private, to promote research and enable them to improve research infrastructure. Establishing a National Research and Innovation Laboratory with access to all educational institutions at the state and central level is important. Incentives can also be provided to empower professors and students for research and development.

Good faculty attracts good research students. We need to attract a world-class research faculty by creating a world-class working environment, re-envisioning salary structures and providing accommodation in universities for possible collaborative international research projects. Universities should identify national challenges and direct their research towards finding innovative solutions. Every university should set up the PURA Cluster Research Centre for traditional research and development for local application for agriculture, industry and service sectors at the village level.

Healthcare Services and Institutions: More medical colleges should be allowed to start, provided they adopt government hospitals and invest in its infrastructure and health service and also adopt at least a hundred village PHCs (Public Health Centres) in their neighbourhood. Medical teaching may also be imparted through high-definition tele-education technology by a well-qualified faculty and a medical laboratory for practical applications may be tied up with government hospitals.

Comprehensive medical insurance provided by the government to the unorganized sector needs to be introduced to provide quality healthcare service to the common man. The establishment of inclusive policies to set up manufacturing industries for healthcare implements and diagnostic service equipment is also required. Ensuring that quality healthcare reaches all states equally through PHCs, tertiary care, via telemedicine and also through mobile hospitals should be the primary objective of the nation.

Inclusive Governance

Inclusive governance means governance that is responsive, transparent and corruption free. We need to achieve an Ease of Doing Business index to less than 50 compared to its present level of 132. (China EoDB is 91). Introduction of e-governance with dynamic secure workflow management from top to bottom that connects the President, the Prime Minister, ministries, governors, CMs, state ministries, departments, secretariat, district collectors, village administrative officers and ultimately the people is essential as is the implementation of issuing of national ID to all the citizens.

We also need changes in the Land, Mines and Minerals Act, internal security, police, inclusive industrial reforms, social justice and women's reservation and consider all other pending bills for redefinition with focus on inclusive growth with equitable social justice.

> Enacting inclusive polices for regulatory, corporate and moral governance and improving responsiveness and accountability in government initiatives aims to improve government and public sector effectiveness and citizens' engagement with government. A responsible and accountable anti-corruption Lokpal Bill simultaneously builds value systems in both the family and the society. Enacting a Citizen's Charter as a solemn commitment of the government or public sector institutions for delivery of services to the intended beneficiaries on time and every time is also crucial.

Reduce Poverty, Illiteracy and Crimes Against Women

The following measures may be taken to bring poverty reduction through PURA for 600,000 villages, which will provide employment opportunities and enrich the quality of life in villages. I have also evolved a User Community Pyramid to ensure that the benefits of the sustainable development model reaches the bottom of the pyramid through the productive use of natural resources, the convergence of technologies, and the evolution of innovative socio-economic business models for evolving a happy, prosperous and peaceful society. We have also developed a radar called the Societal Developmental Radar, which not only provides short-term, midterm and long-term targets but also monitors the progress of attributes like access to food and nutrition; access to water, both potable and irrigation; access to healthcare; access to income generation capacity; access to education and capacity building; access to quality power and communication; and access to financial services. This will lead to the intended benefits reaching the bottom of the pyramid.

Skill and knowledge development through state-of-the-art skill training for the youth of the country is also needed. Programmes can be conceived where students from colleges across India would take up a two-month summer internship programme in villages to enhance water and pond conditions and hygiene.

As for women's safety, a value-based education at the school level is essential to build respect towards women. To bring down the rate of crimes, we need to improve police vigilance and put a system in place for immediate FIR on complaints. An SOS call for women may also be introduced through mobile phones or GPS devices.

Inclusive growth-oriented policies will bring equitable, inclusive growth and level socio-economic imbalances in society which will remove socio-economic and political alienation and reduce Naxalist and Maoist tendencies. Developmental politics instead of political politics will also reduce the prevalent bitter political alienation.

Bringing Peace and Prosperity

For containing terrorism and other forms of insurgency in India, we need to evolve the NCET (National Campaign to Eradicate Terrorism).

I believe the time has come when, apart from the multiple agencies forecasting and handling terrorist activities, we also need to evolve an aggressive mission called the NCET, with a mission-oriented integrated management structure, duly passed by the Parliament.

Under the NCET Bill, we need to bring out the following:

- Creation of a unified intelligence agency across the country with latest technological tools and devices, that is empowered to deal with state and central government intelligence agencies under one roof of administration.
- Enactment of a law which will provide stringent punishment and faster justice to the perpetrators of the crime in a time-bound manner.
- Building wider awareness among people in order to work together in identifying these incidents and eliminating these tendencies with transparent procedures that inform and work with intelligence agencies to combat terrorism.
- Implementation of a national citizen ID card for all transactions with government, business and private sectors.

- Reorientation of central and state administrative mechanisms to ensure that development reaches all sections of the society for achieving inclusive growth and to ensure that none in the society feels alienated socially, economically and politically.

I have suggested that the evolution of the NCET mission be based around action-oriented people of highest integrity and competence drawn from multiple functional areas, committed to the vision of eradicating terrorism. We must do this with a great sense of urgency for when evil minds combine, good minds have to work together.

Regional Peace and Prosperity

India should not only work towards bringing sustainable peace and prosperity within its borders but also among its neighbours. India is the second largest democratic nation in the world and its democratic values have been tested for more than six decades. If Vision 2020 has to reap *all* the benefits of development, India has to see that all of its neighbours, particularly the SAARC nations, have attained peace and prosperity under the democratic system. Otherwise cross-border terrorism, Naxalism and Maoism will continue to threaten the very processes of sustaining peace and prosperity. It is the responsibility of India to bring peace and prosperity in the subcontinent through democracy. I suggest that the SAARC nations work together in a way similar to the EU Parliament which works towards promoting regional peace and prosperity.

Unity of Minds

> At this point, I would like to suggest that on a social level, it is necessary to work towards the unity of minds. Indian civilization is a multi-lingual, multi-faith, multi-racial system that has evolved over centuries. The increasing intolerance for the views and lifestyle of others and the expression of this intolerance through lawlessness cannot be justified under any context. All of us have to work hard to respect the rights of every individual. That is the most fundamental of all democratic values, and, I believe, our civilizational heritage—the very soul of our nation.

Let us evolve ourselves into a society that respects and celebrates differences. Let our experts, leaders and institutions show in their words and deeds:

- Tolerance of other people's opinions.
- Tolerance of other people's cultures.
- Tolerance of other people's beliefs.

- Tolerance of other people's styles.
- Tolerance of other people's ideas.

In fact, such an attitude, at the individual and community level, has always been the hallmark of Indian civilization.

Political System in Democracy

A democracy works on the foundation of people's dreams and aspirations. It is not democracy that has to be re-invented; what needs to be re-invented is our political system, with its responsibilities, its obligations and its boundaries.

Here I would like to recall my addresses in the Parliament and my address to the fifteen state legislative assemblies on the mission for the development of states. I gave them an equation:

Political system = Political politics + Developmental politics.

Any parliamentarian or legislator has to go through these two political components. Political politics focuses on election and electoral politics, that is, getting elected with a declared agenda. Developmental politics focuses on the development of the constituency as part of the mission to develop the state, and thereby, the nation. This requires vision, measurable mission targets, feedback on progress, and even midcourse corrections whenever necessary. I believe that a member, once elected, should spend only 30 per cent of his time on political politics and the remaining 70 per cent on development politics.

The mission has to be to make the constituency a developed one. The parameters for this are:

1. A constituency free from poverty and crime and where the dignity of every human life in ensured in an unbiased manner.
2. A constituency free from illiteracy with state-of-the-art skill development and higher education for the youth.
3. Value-added employment for all with enhanced per capita income.
4. Provision of healthcare services to every citizen and eradication of diseases like TB, cholera, malaria, HIV/AIDS and leprosy. Mass screening and provision of proactive healthcare system leading to reduction in IMR, MMR and chronic diseases.
5. Working towards the creation of enduring infrastructure for safe drinking water, drainage, sanitation, irrigation, transportation, power and enhancing the tourism potential of the constituency.
6. Making the process of administration efficient, transparent and corruption free, so that every citizen feels comfortable in receiving the services without any hassle and can contribute towards national development.

7. Making the constituency a better place to live in, in terms of all the aspects above, so that there is a possibility of reverse migration.
8. In essence, the constituency should have sustainable development with a protected environment which will make the elected leader a friend, philosopher and guide of each and every family of the constituency.

I would also like to suggest some areas where the constituency development fund can be used. Members of Parliament are eligible for allocation of constituency development fund (MPLADS) of ₹5 crore every year. This fund can be used for important infrastructural activities, which will be beneficial to the citizens of the constituency. Some of the programmes which can be implemented through this fund could be:

1. Identifying the water bodies in the constituency that need desilting and opening of the inlet and outlet. Whenever there is rain, only the desilted tanks will be filled up and the level of the ground water in the region will increase. Linking up the water bodies in the constituency is also a possibility.
2. Education for girls needs the highest priority. Some of the major reasons why girls are not sent to school is the non-availability of toilets and the distance of the school from the village. There are many schools with just a single room. MPs and MLAs can assist the existing school to improve infrastructure or start schools in the constituency with child-

friendly infrastructure.

3. A survey of PHCs can be conducted to ensure that the centre is provided with doctors and minimum supporting staff along with equipment and medicines. Funds for tele-medicine connectivity between PHCs and the district hospital in the region can be allocated which will enable access to quality healthcare to the citizens.

4. For providing medical care to the remote areas of the constituency, provision of well-equipped mobile hospitals could be considered which will go to different villages of the constituency on specified dates, so that the patients can be treated in the village itself.

5. Development of state-of-the-art skill in welding, construction, repair and maintenance of electronic equipments will provide value-added employment to the youth. Special courses for the youth of the constituency can be organized for them to acquire skills in polytechnics or ITI located in the constituency or the district headquarters. This would be a great opportunity to create a global cadre of skilled people.

6. Organizing street plays in the constituency depicting the social evils such as dowry, corruption, female foeticide, gender inequality, child marriage and corruption can also be organized, so that the citizens of the constituency are made aware and facilitated to improve their societal characteristics. This will be a great opportunity to create a value-based system.

The message that I am trying to convey is that a democracy with developmental politics has to be the focus of our parliamentary system, since the nation is bigger than the political system.

What Will I Be Remembered For?

Finally, I would like to ask every reader one question: what would you like to be remembered for? You have to evolve and shape your own life. You should write your goal down on a piece of paper. That page might just be a very important page in the book of human history. And you will be remembered for creating that page in the history of the nation—whether that is a page of invention, of innovation, of discovery, of creating societal change, of removing poverty, of fighting injustice or planning and executing a mission for energy independence. And I will be happy if you could mail me this page of yours at apj@abdulkalam.com

I have a message of courage for you. We need this courage to realize our dreams of a happy, safe and prosperous nation.

Courage to think differently,
Courage to invent,
Courage to discover the impossible,
Courage to travel on an unexplored path,
Courage to share knowledge,
Courage to remove pain,
Courage to reach the unreached,

Courage to combat problems
And succeed,
Are the unique qualities of youth.
As the youth of my nation, I will work and work with courage to achieve success in all my missions.